WHAT OTHERS ARE SAYING ABOUT THE HAPPY DANCE

I highly recommend *THE Happy Dance*. Dr. and Mrs. Sloan show great courage in vulnerably sharing their powerful testimony. Phil, a successful pastor and clinical psychologist; and Debby, a successful women's mentor, and interior designer, insightfully teach Scripturally anchored principles of living victoriously in spirit, soul, and body. The beauty of the book is that it combines Spiritual and psychological insights. The Holy Spirit uses these to promote healing and transformation for God's glory and our inner peace. *THE Happy Dance* is not just a delightful read; it is a book through which the Holy Spirit speaks into our life. The Lord has likely drawn you to this book. Reading it will draw you closer to Him.

—BRENT PATTERSON
M. Div. (Marriage and Family Ministries),
Ph.D., Licensed Clinical Psychologist

This book is a must-read for anyone that has been emotionally or spiritually wounded or for those that wish to help someone that has been. It is raw, real, honest, and easy to read and apply to your life. It is not a book that just outlines what you need to do to be victorious but illustrates how to achieve the healing, freedom, peace, and victory so many are searching for. The authors of this book applied these principles to my life by revealing to me the forgiveness of Jesus Christ, the love of God, and the healing of The Holy Spirit. These revelations transformed me from a pew warmer in the back row of the church to a leader of warriors in God's Army. This book belongs on every reading list and in every library. It won't be a one-time read.

—LEE CRAIG
California Coordinator
Point Man International Ministries Inc. (Retired)

Dr. Phil and Debby Sloan have been my friends for years. I vouch for the credibility of both of them. I love the work they have done with *THE Happy Dance*. It will make you laugh, it will make you cry, but more than that, it will make you think. You will find yourself saying: "I can definitely identify with that." I couldn't put it down. I read it through almost in one sitting.

—MIKE D. ROBERTSON
Lead Pastor, Visalia First
Author of several books including,
Dealing With Difficult People

Everyone wants to be happy. For most people, true happiness is circumstantial, biochemical, socioeconomic, temporary, fragile, and sadly—elusive. In my experience, most literature around the subject of happiness seeks a mind-over-matter approach, where we are taught elaborate methods of compartmentalizing our pain while congruently psyching up our minds to a simulated faux happiness. This has always felt inauthentic to me. In *THE Happy Dance*, Dr. Phil and Debby Sloan have charted a biblically-based path to enduring happiness. Phil and Debby communicate with tremendous vulnerability their own path to happiness through the mine field of real-life pain, trauma, and disappointment. Rarely have I encountered a book that so personally challenged me to transcend a mundane, contrived, heavy-laden existence to align with God's gentle call on my soul to celebrate, laugh, and truly live as He created me to be! If you desire to break through to real joy, read this book!

—CRAIG CUNNINGHAM
Lead Pastor, Shadow Rock Church

Dr. Phil & Debby did an incredible job writing this book! No matter your age, IQ or what season in life you find yourself; this book is for you! We all want to experience freedom and enjoy *THE Happy Dance* but many times we are paralyzed and don't realize it! This book is full of wisdom and revelation! You will find yourself re-reading this book as you go through different seasons in life and it will impact you each time you read it! It's time to get your dancing shoes on!

—STEPHANY (GEMME) BENING
Teacher and Speaker

If you desire to find the true, abundant life that God offers you, read this book. In its pages is a wealth of important transformational principles. Presented in a fresh and unique way from an incredible storehouse of experience and relationship with Jesus, the Sloan's have put together a book that is a must-read for those of us who have unknowingly settled for far less than God's gift to us provides. The joy of the Lord truly can be our strength, rather than merely a scripture we've quoted, it can be a way of life.

THE Happy Dance has already helped to reshape some of the foundational ways that I approach my relationship with God: Understanding that my triune being (spirit, soul, and body) is responding to His awesome Triune magnificence (God the Father, God the Son and God the Holy Spirit). Wow, that is a game-changer!

From the same God who caused John The Baptist to leap and dance for joy in utero, I can hear the Heavenly Father, the Lord of the Dance, bidding me, "May I have this dance?" The answer is a joyous, YES!

I pray this book will help you examine yourself and lead you into the astounding liberty that will help you to enjoy the wonderful rhythms of *THE Happy Dance*.

—DAVID GEORGE
Musician, Song Writer,
Executive Pastor and Worship Leader, Waxahachie First

VICTORIOUS LIVING
SPIRIT · SOUL · BODY

DR. PHIL & DEBBY SLOAN

© Copyright 2022 — Phil Sloan

All rights reserved. This book is protected by the laws of the United States of America. This book may not be copied or reprinted for commercial gain or profit. The use of short quotations or occasional page copying for personal or group study is permitted and encouraged. Permission may be granted upon request. Unless otherwise identified, Scripture quotations are from the New International Version of the Bible. Certain pronouns in Scriptures that refer to the Father, Son, and Holy Spirit, are capitalized, and may differ from some Bible publishers' style.

Edited by David George

Cover Design by Katie Mattiuzzo

Published by Printopya, Redding, California

Printed in the United States of America
ISBN 978-0-578-32364-0

Special Appreciation

Without the encouragement of our son, Brent, and our niece, Stephany Bening—there would be no book. Brent, with his creativity and sense of humor, inspired and pushed us through the whole process. He also spent countless hours improving and editing the manuscript. Steph has been a bright light when our vision would become dim. She was our encourager and has taught the principles in this book to other women. Everyone needs cheerleaders. Thank you, thank you!

We want to thank our good friend, David George, for contributing to this work by editing, making suggestions, and being so supportive.

Above all, we are incredibly grateful to our Lord for drawing us to learn and experience the transformation of our lives. We want to thank our "Good, good Heavenly Father" for teaching us to dance!

Table of Contents

Introduction xi
Prologue xvii
Chapter One: *Average is NOT Normal!* 1
Chapter Two: *Choose to Celebrate!* 19
Chapter Three: *"May I Have This Dance?"* 45
Chapter Four: *Are You Out of Your Mind?* 63
Chapter Five: *Pull It Down!* 83
Chapter Six: *Adulterous Emotions* 103
Chapter Seven: *The Body Keeps Score!* 129
Chapter Eight: *It Tastes Sooo Good!* 155
Chapter Nine: *Choose This Day* 183
Chapter Ten: *Who Holds the Deed?* 205
Chapter Eleven: *A Day of Delight A Fresh Beginning!* 227
Epilogue 249

Introduction

Our transition from Bible college to actual church ministry was a culture shock. Our idealistic vision was soon interrupted when we were confronted with problems that were not part of our training. We soon discovered that ministry was more complicated because many people had tremendous knowledge of the Bible but did not know how to handle "life"—life with its hurts, pain, and inner struggles. At that time, we developed a hunger to see individuals changed and transformed into vibrant worshippers and followers of Christ. Not hearers only—but doers—actually living out Biblical principles in their daily life!

My wife, Debby, loves to do puzzles. There is nothing more discouraging than when you are in the final stages of completing the puzzle and discovering pieces missing. Where are they? Were they lost? Were they never in the box from the beginning? It doesn't matter—the result is the same. Without the missing pieces, you cannot complete the project.

From the perspective of a pastor and psychologist and through decades of loving and working with people, we have uncovered some "missing pieces". These are pieces that can bring freedom—freedom to our spirit, soul, and body!

The story that I *(Phil)* share in this book has led me to discover *"THE Happy Dance!"* My dream would be that someone would pick up this book, and I would be able to save them from years—or even a lifetime—of being "frozen in time!" This book contains the "missing pieces" that could help you experience "real" life!

My personal experience of *"THE Happy Dance"* was a culmination of releasing the residue of pain that had laid dormant in my spirit, soul, and body. The wounds of my spirit affected my relationship with God. I was unable to experience His love and freedom fully. The wounds of my soul left me "frozen in time," where I was unable to fully feel, express, and enjoy my relationship with God and others. My amygdala, the brain's emotional center, had been wounded from childhood and everyday life experiences. Life moved on, but part of me remained frozen—"frozen in time".

I did not understand how deeply the wounds of the spirit and soul affect the body. The body is God's design in creation—and it is an essential part of God's plan.

The spirit/soul/body connection is vital to Biblical truth. Like the Holy Trinity (God the Father, Jesus the Son, and the Holy Spirit), our triad—our spirit, soul, and body—is designed to function in unity. The fall of man brought about a negative human triad—fear, shame, and pain. As a result of the fall, the spirit, soul, and body became unaligned. Jesus came to align our being.

Introduction

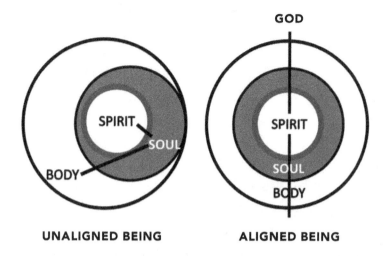

UNALIGNED BEING   **ALIGNED BEING**

Jesus came to heal the brokenhearted and set the captive free. He desires to transform the human negative triad of fear, shame, and pain into one of faith, hope, and healing.

After decades of helping people, Debby and I have discovered that everyone has a battle with this negative human triad. And most have not been made aware of the freedom that can be experienced in *"THE Happy Dance!"*

This book looks at our human triad—our spirit, soul, and body—and reveals steps toward our transformation—back to the way God created us. People have been stunted in their spiritual development and growth by hidden wounds and buried painful life experiences. These painful experiences have impacted: marriages, family relationships, social interactions, church life, vocations, and ministry.

We were in the process of putting the finishing touches and details on this book when our world was turned upside down. I *(Debby)* received a call from the prison where Phil was working. The prison's hospital informed me that Phil was being transported by ambulance to the local hospital. A prisoner had violently attacked him. These attacks are not unusual among the prisoners, and attacks are often directed at the correctional officers. But at this prison, no attack had ever been perpetrated upon the medical staff.

When I arrived at the local hospital, the Warden, the Assistant Warden, and the Chief of Mental Health greeted me with great concern. When I was ushered into Phil's room, I was unprepared to see the physical manifestations of the assault. Phil's face was bruised and swollen. What was just as concerning was for him to relay the event through tears and anxiety.

It was a typical day at my office in the prison's medical ward when I *(Phil)* received a call from the Chief of Mental Health to do an emergency psychological evaluation of an inmate. I interviewed the inmate who was sullen and non-communicative. I then asked the custody staff to return him to his hospital bed. I proceeded to finish my evaluation of this inmate while enjoying the delicious lunch that Debby had prepared for me. As I was eating, I heard a noise at my office door. I looked up, expecting to see an officer or a nurse, but, instead, the inmate had escaped from custody and burst through my door. As I stood to my feet, he began to assault me. He broke my glasses as he began to pummel my face with his fists. My desk prevented me from landing on the concrete floor. Just writing and reliving this experience provokes strong emotion.

Trauma and anxiety can cause a slow leak in the emotional system that can continue to drain a person of his emotional and spiritual, and physical strength throughout a person's lifetime. We must take intentional steps to plug the leak and heal the wounds. The principles in this book saved my life—keeping me from becoming "frozen in time." These principles provided a blueprint for me to be healed and to be victorious—spirit, soul, and body!

Introduction

I encourage you to read this book if life's trials have wounded you. I especially encourage you to read this book if you have no knowledge of the negative human triad and its impact on your life. We have discovered some key principles that reveal how people who have been "frozen in time" can thaw out and enjoy new freedoms.

Prologue

Everyone has a story!

When Debby and I got married, we thought we had bought tickets for life's Merry-Go-Round ride! As a couple, we already had our life all planned out. But God gave us tickets instead for a crazy and wild roller coaster ride! We did not realize that life could be a lot more fun and exhilarating when it is not so predictable! The bumps and jolts from the roller coaster provide more views, more thrills, and greater awareness of the surroundings. From the roller coaster, you are enthralled with all of the new sights, and sounds, and thrills—instead of going around and around seeing the same scenery atop a stationary and lifeless carousel horse.

I have pastored wonderful churches, worked with foster children, and now have the privilege of being a licensed clinical psychologist in the California State Prison System. Debby has owned an interior design business, led women's ministry, and continues to mentor women. We are still amazed by the varied and wonderful experiences that God had planned.

At 22 and 19, we never could have imagined the exciting journeys with its bumps, bruises, and joyful exhilarations that God had planned when He exchanged our tickets. Because our God is sovereign—you may never know what kind of wild ride God has designed for you. But you can be assured that His plan is best and more fulfilling than you could ever have dreamed!

It took us a long time to learn the intricate steps of *"THE Happy Dance!"* and we can hardly wait to learn new steps to this dance. The steps may change, but the spirit of the dance will always remain the same! We want to be *further transformed* and *even more Victorious* in our *spirit, soul, and body!*

On a side note, as a child, I was afraid of roller coasters.

Chapter One

Average is NOT Normal!

In my early ministry as a pastor, I *(Phil)* met with a group of leaders in our church. One of the men who was born and raised in the church and a Bible teacher stated, "I've done this Christian life so long now, I can pretty much do it on my own. There has to be something more!" He was like the rich young ruler in the Bible,[1] who obeyed the scriptures, but he knew something was missing!

He was seeking a *"zoe"* life, an active, vigorous, and devoted to God-life.[2] But this man was actually living a *"bio"* life. He was living his life by his *own* biblical and ethical abilities but was crying out for his life to be *transformed* (*"zoe life"*).

As a lead pastor for over thirty years, I have come to a very enlightened, howbeit discouraging insight. Many church member's lives look very much like their non-Christian but morally upright next-door neighbors' lives. Yes, they desire a love for God and others, but many church members' choices reveal their self-interests come first. Their priorities and the way their day is ordered appear to be no different than their next-door neighbor. They are living with the same anxious thoughts and worries. They often react in the same way to discouraging news and events. They are living like the average American—expecting so much more but eventually settling for so much less—even in their spiritual life.

Is God the "director" of their life each moment of the day? Or is He relegated to be an occasional "spiritual consultant"?

Maybe that is the reason that God allows difficulties to come into our life. He wants to make us aware that we desperately need Him. We run to Him with our need, but unfortunately, we often go back to taking charge of our own life.

But the *transformed* life of a *zoe* (normal) Christian demonstrated in the Word of God is strikingly different than that of the *"bio"* or lukewarm Christian. In the life of a *transformed* Christian, selfishness and self-centeredness have given way to generosity and sacrificial giving. Reactions and responses are now loving and God-infused. There is peace and calm when everything goes wrong. There is joy even in difficult circumstances. The *zoe* (normal) Christian is growing in self-control and courage, in gratitude and humility. God is at the forefront of every decision. Thought processes and emotions are being brought under the control of the Holy Spirit. The Holy Spirit is *transforming* their thinking, feelings, and behaviors.

This transformation is the life God has made possible—and the life that He wants for us. We shouldn't settle for anything less! Now that is Biblical *Victorious* living—and how sad that is not the norm(al)! We have substituted a different standard than the one given to us in the New Testament. Too often, we feel spiritually defeated and simply give up.

TRANSFORMATION

Life has a way of building walls faster than we are able to tear down. Often, even a leader may look and talk like a mighty warrior, but deep inside they are just a hurt child who needs their Heavenly Father's love and healing grace.

LIFE HAS A WAY OF BUILDING WALLS FASTER THAN WE ARE ABLE TO TEAR DOWN!

Like a city that is broken into and without walls is a man who has no control over his spirit.

—PROVERBS 25:28

These vivid words come from a man named Solomon. Solomon had allowed his own walls of wisdom to be penetrated and broken. Solomon had allowed his bodily appetites and his ambitions to dominate his soul. Even though he was known for his great wisdom, Solomon was blinded by pleasure-seeking and his lust for power.

The spiritual freedom that Jesus provides is not a license or the right to do whatever you want. It is the freedom to do what you *need* to do in order to experience real *zoe* life. It is the freedom from being driven by your selfish desires.

If you do not see a need for or allow for Christ's continual *transformation*, you will be just like your morally upright but spiritually blinded, next-door neighbor. *Transformation* is an on-going process of change. Christ, the Eternal Sculptor, wants to chisel away at your hardened stony heart, making you into His image–reproducing His heart, His mind, and His character within you.

Transformation requires passion and effort. You might say that you don't have that kind of energy right now because you are barely coping with life. But if you aren't willing to put in the time and energy now, you will become depleted and have even less energy later. Your account will build and even mushroom!

TRANSFORMATION REQUIRES PASSION AND EFFORT.

General William Booth (1829-1916), the founder of the Salvation Army, declared, "The chief dangers which confront the coming century (today!) will be religion without the Holy Ghost, Christianity without Christ, forgiveness without repentance, salvation without regeneration (*transformation*), politics without God, heaven without hell."[3] He was speaking with a prophetic warning to *this* generation.

God is concerned with the whole man!

*May God Himself, the God of peace, sanctify you through and through. May your whole **spirit**, **soul**, and **body** be kept blameless at the coming of our Lord Jesus Christ.*
      —1 THESSALONIANS 5:23, Emphasis Added

Spirit—is the most vital part of us; the stronger the spirit becomes, the more influence it has over our soul and body.

Soul—this is what the Bible spends so much time on because it impacts our emotions, motivations, and behaviors—and can even impact our spirit.

Body—is what everybody sees and recognizes. It reflects my spirit and soul. It provides a window that reveals to others the condition and health of my soul and spirit. So, we can't as Christians ignore it—even though there are times we want to!

There are some dynamic Christians like Joni Eareckson Tada—a well-known author, speaker, and quadriplegic artist—who have overcome the temptation of allowing their body's handicap to rule over them. And instead, they have been *transformed* as they have yielded their weakened body to God, demonstrating His overcoming power.

Joni states, "The weaker I am, the harder I must lean on God's grace; the harder I lean on Him, the stronger I discover Him to be, and the bolder my testimony to His grace. God is more concerned with conforming me to the likeness of His Son than leaving me in my comfort zones. God is more interested in inward qualities than outward circumstances—things like refining my faith, humbling my heart, cleaning up my thought life and strengthening my character."[4]

Her testimony has inspired thousands worldwide to overcome discouragement and become stronger in their spirit.

Yes, God wants to sanctify our whole being. He wants to have our spirit, our soul, and our body be *"set apart for Him!"*[5] And when this occurs, we can actually be "blameless"—we are without spot, no fault being found, not being "caught" or "accused"[6]—now that's *Victorious!*

We often get saved and then slip back into old comfortable, and familiar patterns of thought and behavior. We have access to the power of Christ to make us into complete, whole men and women, but God will not bypass our free will. Even that reveals how much He loves us!

WE OFTEN GET SAVED AND THEN SLIP BACK INTO OLD COMFORTABLE, AND FAMILIAR PATTERNS OF THOUGHT AND BEHAVIOR.

As we learn the different functions of our spirit, soul, and body, we will better understand how to cooperate with God, surrender our will, and be made whole and sanctified—spirit, soul, and body.

> *And Jehovah God formed man of the dust of the ground (body) and breathed into his nostrils the breath of life (spirit); and man became a living **soul**.*
> —GENESIS 2:7, ASV, Brackets and Emphasis Added

Do you ever feel fragmented or feel that you are being pulled apart at the seams? That is because we are a triune being (consisting of spirit/soul/body) with three different areas of awareness.

God operates in all of our triune being. Our spirit's awareness and influence are from "God". Our body's awareness and influence are from its contact with the physical "world". This contact begins as an infant feeling hungry and progresses until we mature and our physical body senses danger. Our soul's awareness and influence are "self", and this affects our mind and emotions.[7]

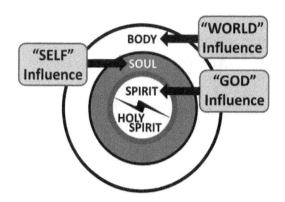

AWARENESS and INFLUENCE of our TRIUNE BEING

Which influences and pressures are going to win out and demand your attention and captivate your focus? Will it be my "self", my "world", or my "God"? Oh, how I yearn just to be God-conscious, but I live in a fallen world with my own fallen nature. I must cooperate; God has the power for my *transformation*, but I must submit my whole triune being to Him and choose *transformation*.

If our "world" awareness and influence cause our soul to feel loneliness, stress, rejection, low self-esteem, fear, frustration, anger, despair, depression, or pleasure—there will be a response, even if we are not aware of it. We can become dominated and driven by those feelings. When these feelings drive us, we have just allowed our "soul" to take charge of our life.

If we do not want to deal with those feelings because they make us uncomfortable, we will try to push them down deep within our soul. We have just chosen to master our life by our logic and understanding, and our "soul" takes charge of our life.

If these two responses don't bring the peace we desire, we often let our bodies dominate and take over our being, and we become body-driven. We then begin to give in to our body's responses, cravings, binges, and habits. And our "body" takes charge of our life—the health-minded begin to over-exercise, the impulsive person begins to overeat or overspend, the workaholic begins to overwork.

THE "ME" GENERATION

We are "fearfully and wonderfully made"—and might I add very complicated! Our culture dramatically changed in the '70s to the "*Me* Generation": "It's all about me!" and "Do your own thing!" and "If it feels good, do it!" These expressions declare that my body and my soul are in control of my life, going against God's original design.

Could it be that this philosophy and attitude has gradually slithered into the church?

COULD IT BE THAT THIS PHILOSOPHY AND ATTITUDE HAS GRADUALLY SLITHERED INTO THE CHURCH?

According to historian Christopher Lasch, Narcissism, named for the Greek god Narcissus, who fell in love with his own reflection in a pool, is the hallmark of the '70s. He has traced the shift from rugged individualism to the so-called "*Me*" Generation.

"What are the signs of this new attitude? The values associated with the work ethic—delayed gratification, self-sacrifice, thrift, and industry—no longer enjoy wide play. The stress is now on the legitimacy of immediate gratification. People want to get in touch with their feelings, eat health food, take lessons in ballet or belly dancing, immerse themselves in the Wisdom of the East, jog, and learn how to relate. Permissive society is in; guilt and punishment are out. Self-help is in; authority is out. Leisure is in; working is out. Spending is in; saving is out. Selling yourself and role-playing are in; craftsmanship is out. Therapy is in; religion is out. Superficiality is in; depth is out. Nonbinding relationships are in; commitments are out."[8]

A devastating event transpired soon after the origin of time when God formed man out of the molecules of the earth and created within his body a soul and a spirit. He wanted to make someone like Himself who could communicate in word and love and actions. He wanted that person to be able to feel the tremendous river of love and joy that comes from being made in the image of God. But as mankind began to experience this glorious freedom, his ability to choose was hijacked by a perilous enemy, the devil. This insidious and malicious liar, who envied what man was given, came to pervert and disrupt the flow of love and joy that had been bestowed freely. A great reversal took place in man when he disobeyed God and fell from this exalted place of joy.

Before the fall of man, the soul was under the control of his spirit. But our trouble started when we decided to reverse that order and allowed our soul and body to rule our life. We now live in a state of confusion. Even within the lives of Christians, there is a war going on. What part of my being is in charge? Which part is going to win this battle?

God dwells and influences our spirit, "self" dwells and influences our soul, and our "senses" dwell and influence our body. Our soul is the middle link, and it can be impacted by either the spirit or the body. The soul houses our personality. The soul dreams, feels, and imagines—it is the place where our emotions live. Our soul also houses our intellect—our thinking and logic.

Our soul needs to be healed and restored because the soul has the final word—it is in control of all our choices and decisions. The soul decides who is going to rule and be in charge of our being—every moment of our lives, for the rest of our lives!

OUR SOUL NEEDS TO BE HEALED AND RESTORED BECAUSE THE SOUL HAS THE FINAL WORD.

Our body is the reflection of our five senses and our soul. The world around us cannot see directly into our soul—our soul's thoughts, imaginations, dreams, or fears—but the *results* of our thoughts, feelings, and choices are on display for all to see. And even by our countenance and by the words that we speak. And by our body's behaviors. They are the manifestation of our soul.

What condition of your soul does the world, your family, friends, neighbors, associates, and even strangers observe? It is your *testimony* to your world!

Does it reflect that the Holy Spirit is inspiring and directing your words and behaviors? Does it reflect peace and order or chaos and compulsion? Does your soul need to be "restored"—back to its original design? When this occurs, it becomes a testimony of God's grace upon our whole life.

The first time that I *(Debby)* ever heard God distinctly speaking in my spirit was when I was a young pastor's wife. My best friend in our church was a dynamic young woman—she was spiritual and an anointed teacher. I had just been asked to teach an adult class for the first time. As I was calling out to God in desperation, I declared, "When I look at Rosemary I feel so insecure in my teaching!" God spoke back to me, "You call it insecurity. I call it envy!" And sure enough, when I thought about my young life, I could see what God meant.

Yes, our God declares that He has a remedy to bring clarity to our confusion and to bring everything back to order.

RESTORATION

He restores my soul; He guides me in the paths of righteousness for His name's sake.

—PSALM 23:3, NASB

That's right—God can heal us and return our soul back to His original design and His holy influence. We are not left drifting on our own on the sea of life without His guidance and direction.

Victorious Living happens when we allow God's Word and His Holy Spirit to powerfully penetrate and influence our entire being (spirit/soul/body)! And this is God's "Normal!"

Solomon was the wisest man to ever walk the earth, except for Jesus Christ. God imbued Solomon's spirit with His supernatural wisdom. But Solomon did not allow his God-inspired spirit to completely rule his being. Even as wise as Solomon was, left to his own devices, he was influenced and flawed by his sinful nature. And he was deceived by his worldly soul. His appetites were out of control and he always wanted more—more horses, more chariots, and even more wives!

His father, David, was known as a man after God's own heart. He had that kind of desire—to love and live the way God does. But even David allowed his selfish soul to sometimes dominate. David writes about his own soul's condition in the book of Psalms. The Psalmist said that his soul: is in "anguish", is "in grief", "is forlorn", "yearns", "faints", "is full of trouble", "is consumed with longing", "faints with longing", "is downcast", "is weary with sorrow", and "disturbed".

David understood that it was not good when his soul was left to its own devices! His soul required adjusting. David learned that his soul needed God's infusion, "… for in You my soul takes refuge" and "my soul finds rest in God alone."

David also experienced that his soul could be "satisfied", "revived", "restored", "redeemed", and "delivered"—by God's Holy influence. And when God restored David's soul, he found that God "brought joy to his soul" and "delivered his soul from death", and even "brought delight to his soul."

WE DESPERATELY NEED HELP!

Isaiah, the ancient prophet, revealed that we are very much like sheep when he stated: "All of us, like sheep, have strayed away. We have left God's paths to follow our own." (Isaiah 53:6, NLT)

But God did not leave us on our own—He sent Jesus to guide us to the path of victory—He is the very Good Shepherd!

> *I am the Good Shepherd; I know My sheep and My sheep know Me—just as the Father knows Me and I know the Father— and I lay down My life for the sheep.*
>
> —JOHN 10:14-15

BUT GOD DID NOT LEAVE US ON OUR OWN—HE SENT JESUS TO GUIDE US TO THE PATH OF VICTORY—HE IS THE VERY GOOD SHEPHERD!

The Good Shepherd gave His life for us; He gave the costliest gift and investment for our future. But He also understood that His sacrifice alone was not enough. He knew that we would need His constant leadership and protection, and He offered to be our guide throughout our life.

We must be willing to follow the Good Shepherd and allow Him to restore our soul. God wants to repair, re-build, and heal—bringing our soul back to its condition as designed at creation.

It is Spiritual *transformation* and it is the only way to *Victorious* Living—spirit, soul, and body! Back to *Victorious* being *normal*!

I am being *TRANSFORMED…*
By Not Settling to Be the Average Christian!

Study Questions

1. Each *moment* of your day is GOD...

   ☐ Your Director   OR   ☐ Your Occasional Spiritual Consultant

   Explain: _____

   _____

   _____

   _____

   _____

2. Read 1 Thessalonians 5:23. How does it make you feel when you read that GOD wants to sanctify our various parts—He wants to have our spirit, our soul, and our body be "set apart for Him"?

   _____

   _____

   _____

   _____

   _____

THE Happy Dance

3. Do you ever feel spiritually defeated and feel like giving up?

   ☐ Yes   OR   ☐ No

   Explain: _____

   _____

   _____

   _____

   _____

4. Do you feel pressure coming from your "world"?

   ☐ Yes   OR   ☐ No

   Explain: _____

   _____

   _____

   _____

   _____

   Does it cause any of the following emotions?

   ☐ Loneliness   ☐ Stress   ☐ Rejection

   ☐ Low Self-Esteem   ☐ Frustration   ☐ Anger

   ☐ Despair   ☐ Depression

5. Are you more prone to be:

    ☐ Driven by these feelings!

    OR

    ☐ Push the feelings down and let logic rule!

6. Are you ever pulled to give into your own body by:

    ☐ Uncontrolled Responses   ☐ Cravings

    ☐ Binges   ☐ Habits

7. Our body is a reflection of our soul—by our behaviors and our words. Does it reflect that the HOLY SPIRIT is inspiring and directing your words and behaviors?

    ☐ Yes   ☐ No   ☐ Sometimes

8. Does your soul need to be restored—back to its original design? Back to the HOLY SPIRIT inspiring your spirit and allowing for your spirit to reign over your soul, and thus, your body.

    ☐ Yes   ☐ No

Chapter Two
Choose to Celebrate!

One morning Phil and I were on one of our fabulous walks together. In the middle of this walk he asked me, "What do you want for Christmas?" As I thought about it, tears began streaming down my face as I told him, "All I want for Christmas is for you to do *THE Happy Dance!*" Phil almost stumbled because he knew exactly what I meant, and he wasn't ready to dance.

A dear friend of mine has many burdens to carry. It seems like it is truly more than she can physically and emotionally bear. I can sense the weight of the oppressing burden on her life, and I respond by joining with her in my own tears. I have empathy and compassion, but at the same time, I know that God does not want her to be this overburdened. She is a giving person—but now has no reserve. She is a caring person—but now can't emotionally reach out. She is a hard worker—but now her energy is spent.

We join together and cry out to God for His solution. And He answers! But His answer is difficult for my dear friend to process. It goes against the standard she has thrust upon herself. It will free her in some areas—so it couldn't possibly be God's will! Isn't His will always restrictive, demanding, and burdensome? How does one shake off their own accusing and judging conscience? That day I told her that my prayer for her was that one day she would pull over to the side of the road, get out of her car and have a *"Happy Dance!"*

I then shared with her our story. After being a pastor for over thirty years, my husband felt that he was to spend the next years of his life ministering to the fatherless. We didn't have a clue what that would look like, but we felt excited about our future. (Who knew that God's plan was for Phil to minister to a prison population that is mainly fatherless!)

Phil and I had lived in the city for eight years and absolutely loved our church. But when God says to move, He gives you grace for the exit, and you lose your strong attachment. We packed our things, the movers came, and we attended our last service. There was sadness and tears, but there was excitement for our future—wondering what is God up to?

Later that day when we left town, I was following my husband in my own car. We were on a seven-hour road trip, heading back to our home in Redding that had never sold and had become a rental. My husband pulled over unexpectedly into a parking lot. Because he was driving his very special twenty-year-old Datsun Z, I thought, oh no, he must be having car trouble. But instead, when he got out of the car, he was beaming from ear to ear—he took my hand and we had a *"Happy Dance"* right there in the parking lot. We were celebrating a fresh beginning—we were leaving worries and concerns behind us. We felt free from consuming responsibilities. We felt free enough to dance right there in a parking lot! This was a dance of celebration—a dance that symbolized that we were trusting God with our future! We didn't know it then, but this moment was a foretaste for things to come. God had more freedoms for us to enjoy and would give us more reasons to kick up our heels.

By the way, my overburdened friend that I previously mentioned, has been able to give her heavy load to God—and she has experienced her own *"Happy Dance!"*

The god of "this world" has an agenda! As he did with Jesus, the devil applies pressure with deceitful trickery. He lures us to run a hundred-meter dash—the fast and furious route—instead of running the distance race with winning endurance. The way of the world—the quick route—promises happiness, satiates us with its desires, and applies pressure to coerce us into its standards. The world is a harsh taskmaster and blindly drives us toward a path of illusive dreams.

THE WORLD IS A HARSH TASKMASTER AND BLINDLY DRIVES US TOWARD A PATH OF ILLUSIVE DREAMS!

In contrast to Satan's plan, Jesus sent us the Holy Spirit to help us find a meaningful and fulfilling life. Often this course seems too slow, but the Holy Spirit dwells within us—in love and patience—to guide us. Not by pressure but by love! His selfless love is a multi-layer pattern designed to be woven into our spirit.

When we receive salvation, all three elements of man's spirit are involved and awakened! The Holy Spirit quickened our human spirit, and we sensed a "Spiritual Knowing". This revelation told us "There really is a God!" Having grasped this personal revelation, our own spirit's "Spiritual Conscience" awakens, and we recognize "I have sinned!"

> *For all have sinned and fall short of the glory of God.*
> —ROMANS 3:23

With this personal admission, we are ready for our soul to respond to the Good News. And now, by asking Jesus into our heart, we receive salvation, making it possible for our spirit to have "Spiritual Union" with the Holy Trinity—God the Father, Jesus Christ His Son, and His Holy Spirit. We may not know it then, but this has become the best day of our life!

At our salvation, the blood of Jesus Christ has finally silenced our own conscience's condemning voice. And now our own spirit's "Spiritual Knowing" is ignited—now we can hear God's voice declare, *"You are forgiven!"* Now the Holy Spirit can speak clearly to us and our own "Spiritual Conscience."

God states that He goes before you and will never leave you nor forsake you. But He doesn't stop there! When we receive Jesus Christ as our Savior, the Holy Spirit comes to live within our human spirit.

When we fail to recognize the Holy Spirit's presence or ignore His prompting, we do not allow the Holy Spirit to *transform* and influence our life. God transforms, but we must participate! So often I *(Debby)* have become complacent and have settled for so much less. At times I have chosen to live under the influence and counsel of my selfish soul when I could have been experiencing the same mindset of Christ Jesus! Imagine the ability to think His thoughts, say His words, and do His deeds! How is that even feasible or possible? It is possible because the Holy Spirit's purpose is: to reveal to us, to guide us, to teach us, and to communicate—the very essence and the reality of Christ.

GOD TRANSFORMS, BUT WE MUST PARTICIPATE!

The Holy Spirit gives us the ability to understand the holy realm of God. And only with this understanding can we truly know the intents and purposes of God!

The Spirit of the Lord will rest on Him—the Spirit of wisdom and understanding, the Spirit of counsel and of might, the Spirit of the knowledge and fear of the Lord.
—ISAIAH 11:2

Our human spirit is the receptor of receiving the Holy Spirit into our lives. God desires to give us fresh understanding and knowledge. However, it requires that our whole being be *teachable*—that is we must desire *transformation*! We must desire to want to live by God's design!

Being teachable requires humility—recognizing our own vulnerabilities and weaknesses. Being teachable also requires being sensitive to God's Word and His direction. We then must be willing to make any necessary changes. We must choose a lifestyle that is totally surrendered—spirit, soul, and body. It is a lifestyle that wants to learn and adopt new truths, concepts, and even new habits! This lifestyle does not prefer the automatic or old preferences. We must let those die and be open to learning a new and *Victorious* way of thinking, feeling, and responding.

SPIRITUAL "KNOWING"

God breathed into man the breath of life, awakening man's spirit. Of our human triune being—spirit, soul, and body—it is in our spirit where the Holy Spirit takes up residence in a believer's life. At our salvation, our human spirit has the potential to once again come under the holy influence of God. Our spirit, like God's Spirit, has a sensing mechanism.

From our spirit, we recognized God, and we were drawn to the Lord and desired salvation from our sins. Salvation wasn't our own idea—it was a God-idea infused into our spirit.

God has equipped our spirit to be a receptor of His Holy influence—it is "Spiritual Knowing".

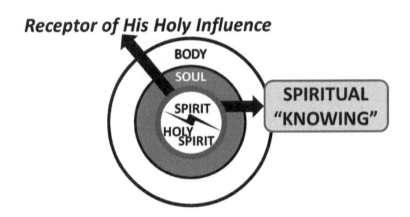

Like our soul, our spirit also *senses*—thoughts, desires, and feelings from deep within. Spiritual maturity comes when we learn to discern between our own natural senses and those coming from divine inspiration! Our natural senses have an external origin—it was produced by nouns (people, places, and things) or by events.[9] Our natural senses are a reaction.

But our "Spiritual Knowing" is not an emotional response—it comes without cause and effect[10] from deep within our spirit. It reflects the attitudes, thoughts, and the mind of God. It has nothing to do with our own mind, emotion, and will. It is the "Holy Spirit's Knowing" inspiring "our" spirit to have "Spiritual Knowing".

As humans, our natural senses are processed through our mind, and our mind yearns to understand. Our spirit does not need to come to that understanding—it just "Knows." For instance, when we receive salvation, our spirit "Knows" that there is a God even though it may not be able to be proven to our own mind's satisfaction. Our spirit "Knows"—because the Holy Spirit speaks to us and operates in our spirit!

The Spirit Himself testifies with our spirit that we are God's children.

—ROMANS 8:16

SKIPPING DOWN FERGUSON ROAD!

I *(Debby)* was standing during the worship segment at my church's women's Bible study. The presence of God was very near me at that moment, and I sensed God's voice speak to my spirit very distinctly. He said, *"I want you to celebrate!"* His words would not leave my heart or mind. I knew these words had a deep meaning, so I immediately sat down and wrote them on a leaflet in my Bible. I did not want to forget these important words when the busyness of my day bombarded my mind. I was greatly moved and could hardly wait to see what God meant!

I WANT YOU TO CELEBRATE!

Later that day, I decided to take a walk where I could talk to God without any distractions. When I inquired of God, "What did you mean? What am I to celebrate?" He responded in my spirit, "I want you to celebrate *all* of the life that I chose for you."

I then realized I didn't understand what He meant by "celebrate!" So, I asked God, "What exactly do you mean? I don't understand!" Often, I grasp the meaning of words better by looking at their opposites. Knowing this about me God spoke to my spirit, *"Celebrate is the opposite of mourning."*

That is when, in my mind, I saw a mental picture of me in a hole; it was really a shallow grave. An image of me experiencing each difficulty in my life flashed before my eyes. As these images would appear, I saw a layer of a light dusting of dirt on top of me. I reacted by shaking off the dirt, but a new layer of dirt had appeared when I tried to get up. No matter how many times I shook the dirt off, I could not get up.

Grief and hurt will bury you alive! I was in a hole and couldn't get up because of the dirt that was restricting me. The dirt represented layers of sorrow, pride, self-pity, and anger. I couldn't move forward or jump for joy because I was lifeless in a hole of "self". I was removed from deep intimacy with God and others because of the layers of "self".

GRIEF AND HURT WILL BURY YOU ALIVE!

Then God said, *"Now, instead of grieving over each difficulty, choose to celebrate each one! Choose to celebrate because I called you to this life. Choose to celebrate My plan—you have always just accepted it! Choose to celebrate it!"*

I declared out loud, yes, for all to hear, "I choose to celebrate, I *choose* to celebrate, I *choose to celebrate*! And as I did, in my mind I saw myself jumping out of that shallow grave, leaving all the dusting residue of my mourning behind.

With my new-found freedom, I found myself skipping down Ferguson Road! Yes, that's right—a more than middle-aged woman skipping down the street. It was *"THE Happy Dance!"* My emotions no longer bound me, and there was a spring in my step all the way home! I had been in the presence of my God, and He was affirming, correcting, and healing me all at the same time! How could I *not* "Celebrate"?

David described my heart's condition:

When my heart was grieved and my spirit embittered, I was senseless and ignorant; I was a brute beast before You. Yet I am always with You; You hold me by my right hand. You guide me with Your counsel.

—PSALM 73:21-24

God counseled me to rejoice and celebrate His path. I found my "missing piece!" And this is the outcome:

I will turn their mourning into gladness; I will give them comfort and joy instead of sorrow.

—ISAIAH 31:13

God gave me a very tight rope that day. I realized that if I am choosing *not* to celebrate, I could easily go back to my old pattern of mourning! David described this state of mind:

When my prayers returned to me unanswered, I went about mourning.

—PSALM 35:13-14

Mourning is about "me!" Celebrating is about "Him!"

I have always been a positive and happy person, but even more so, since I had that divine encounter on Ferguson Road. I chose to participate in my spiritual *transformation*—I now have a deeper joy than I have ever known. It is not transitory or fleeting. It is not contingent upon anything. It is freedom from grief and regret! It is pure joy!

And oh, how I wanted this same gift for my husband.

One of the blessings of being married is sharing the same experiences and history with your mate. You don't have to explain events—you were there together. I was there when the doctor unexpectedly shared the difficult news that Phil could not have children. I did not have a clue that day, how those words would impact the rest of our lives. I knew pain that day, but I did not know how that pain would change throughout the years. I did not know that pain can change in its appearance or condition. I did not know about the metamorphosis of pain.

A few years later after our devastating news, I was able to experience a powerful and supernatural healing of my emotions regarding this painful trauma. The Lord sent someone who showed me how to let go of the hurt and pain, and I began a process of learning to trust God. Baby showers and maternity clothes were no longer a catalyst for sadness because I had been so healed. I could sincerely rejoice with others and not feel envy for the news of a new baby being born. It was so freeing!

Phil is such a spiritual and godly man—I did not think that he had any residual issues regarding this loss. Yes, I knew that he was devastated with the news, but I presumed that he had eventually given it all to God and had completely dealt with his loss. I did not know that he had taken it so very personally—with hidden ramifications of self-guilt and condemnation. I did not know that he blamed himself. I did not know that he took on my pain as well as his own. I did not know for many decades.

We were on a road trip and having a very deep and spiritual conversation. And then, from out of the blue, Phil asked me a very shocking question. He asked if I could ever forgive him. "Forgive you for what?" I asked. And he responded, "For keeping you from having children." I was shocked and stunned. I thought all of those old feelings and emotions had been dealt with decades before. I had never blamed Phil—I had blamed God! But here he was emotionally expressing deep pain—and his concern was for me! His question was penetrating and revealing. Phil thought I had not forgiven him, because really, he could not forgive himself. For what?

BROKEN STONES, BROKEN DREAMS

It was a few weeks before Christmas and I *(Phil)* was asking my wife about a special gift. She surprised me with this comment, "All I want for Christmas is for you to do *'THE Happy Dance!'*" Wow! That may seem simple to some, and others might think I got by real lucky. But for me, this was a critical step in the process of healing from past wounds and life experiences.

ALL I WANT FOR CHRISTMAS IS FOR YOU TO DO "THE HAPPY DANCE!"

It was very challenging for me to go back to the roots of my pain and to understand why it had never been totally resolved. In thinking back at the age of 25 and hearing the doctor tell me that I had zero sperm count, I believe psychologically I had buried it in denial. But I also wanted to have great faith that miracles could happen and someday I would have children. After all, I grew up hearing about Abraham and Sarah, and how God overruled barrenness. Even though I was thriving in my role as a pastor, I was very immature in knowing how to handle all the devilish thoughts that would come, and continue to come, for decades. Looking back now, I can see that Satan developed a "Stronghold" in me. And he would use it when needed, at strategic times and places in my life.

I had never battled or questioned my masculinity. While growing up, I did not understand what real manhood involved. Even though my father was a strong and ambitious man, he didn't possess other attributes that now I understand God desires in a man. I feared his wrath and felt his disapproval, and he began to be an image of a father. I understood the wrath of a father, but I was unable to experience and understand the love of a father. And until I learned differently, this attitude was transferred to my Heavenly Father.

When I was told that I could never father children, I immediately experienced the insidious whisper of Lucifer saying you are inferior and incomplete. My masculinity was under attack. I was not equipped in the depths of my soul to refute the malicious lies.

Intellectually, I understood the biblical concept of manhood, but there was painful confusion down in my innermost private sanctuary. And as the emasculation began, I was not prepared to acknowledge or deal with the painful process that was germinating inside me—affecting my soul and body.

When I was in college preparing for ministry, I commuted with a mature student who appeared to have a great knowledge of the Bible. He loved the Old Testament and talked about the required qualifications for ministry in the Levitical priesthood. My friend's reference to having "broken stones" really stuck in my mind. He was sincerely sowing seed, but little did he know that the enemy would use these seeds to condemn and bring bondage to my soul! As we know from the temptation of Christ, one of the devil's craftiest tools is to use the Word of God.

AS WE KNOW FROM THE TEMPTATION OF CHRIST, ONE OF THE DEVIL'S CRAFTIEST TOOLS IS TO USE THE WORD OF GOD.

> *For whatever man he is who has a blemish, he shall not approach: a blind man, or a lame... or has his stones broken; no man of the seed of Aaron the priest, who has a blemish, shall come near to offer the offerings of Yahweh made by fire. He has a blemish.*
>
> —LEVITICUS 21:18

My colleague interpreted this scripture to mean that this man could not reproduce and therefore was not fit for ministry! I had great admiration for this man and could not know that his words would come back to haunt me. In my insecurity, his teaching would challenge my feelings of masculinity and manhood. When the doctor said I had no sperm count, those words began to torment me!

It is very challenging for me and a bit distressing to explain the process that germinated in the deep recesses of my inner being.

In the church world, we were finding success, especially given our age and experience. Because I was so busy, I was not aware that I was burying my pain. And that pain was in a process of migrating into another arena of my life.

Despite the fresh blessings pouring into our lives, there was stirring inside of me a lack of total trust in God's providence. My "blemish" was not being erased. At different times without my awareness of what was taking place, my "blemish" would rear its ugly head. I thought that I had adjusted and moved on, but lingering doubts still plagued me.

Every time that one of our friends announced their pregnancy, it was like opening an old wound. I struggled when I would see young unwed mothers who did not even want a child to become pregnant. I wondered "Why, God? What is so wrong with me that you cannot reverse this curse? After all, I am serving You with all my heart and doing whatever I can to build Your kingdom." But things remained the same as I focused on my work and experienced success.

The seed of God's Word had been planted in truth. But my interpretation of it was eventually mixed with poison that would germinate an unhealthy seed and bring great pain. My spiritual hunger and zeal would become a stomping ground for an unholy dance until *"THE Happy Dance"* could prevail!

I had a picture in my mind that I would be a successful pastor with a lovely wife, three wonderfully behaved children, and the admiration of those I served. I had the lovely wife, at times admiration, but my dream was not God's dream for me—it was mine. So, I kicked myself for years for being blemished and the one to blame for that dream not taking fruition. After all, doesn't God think as I do?

GREAT EXPECTATIONS!

In reflecting back over our past adventures in life, I realize that one of the reasons I was able to bury my pain was because my life was filled with so many good things. I had been able to pastor great churches and experience a significant amount of growth and blessings. We were able to go into difficult situations of debt and despair and see the *transformation* of people and God's miraculous provision in so many ways. Debby and I were also able to work together in a megachurch and grow in many areas of vision and ministry. My life was favored by God, and I was a recipient of many of the things I had dreamed about when I entered full-time ministry.

During these busy times, I always had a dream of being not only a pastor but also a psychologist. I was accepted into a doctoral program, and upon completion, I have been able to work for the State of California in the Prison System. And now, I have been able to share God's love and help many prisoners after retiring from full-time pastoring.

Even though I have been blessed in so many ways, I do not want to minimize the pain we go through when we carry the toxic poison of deceitful lies within us. These lies come from our adversary, the devil, who has been defined as "the accuser of the brethren."[11] That insidious voice of accusation that has been submerged in our subconscious will emerge for more significant harm during times of stress and crisis. That is exactly what transpired in my life while living in Portland, Oregon. You have heard the Charles Dickens' saying, "It was the best of times; it was the worst of times."

THAT INSIDIOUS VOICE OF ACCUSATION THAT HAS BEEN SUBMERGED IN OUR SUBCONSCIOUS WILL EMERGE FOR GREATER HARM DURING TIMES OF STRESS AND CRISIS.

PAIN OF A FATHER'S HEART!

Portland, Oregon, is a beautiful city placed on the site of two adjoining rivers. It was a beautiful place to live, and we were anticipating great things as we arrived in that city. It was not the beauty of the area that enthralled us, but rather the people who had requested us to be their pastors.

Living in Portland was the beginning of a great adventure for our family. We were able to buy a great home with views of snow-capped mountains. We had a beautiful church facility, that had a fantastic location right on the corner of a busy thoroughfare.

One of the great blessings of our time in Portland was when our adopted son, Brent, came to join us. He had just completed a program in Teen Challenge, a Christ-centered drug addiction rehabilitation program. He gave his testimony, and we shared together in an illustrated sermon entitled "Rebound." He worked at the church and even began a ministerial course that would qualify him to be a licensed minister. He eventually became a youth pastor at another church in the area and was engaged to a wonderful young woman who shared his passion for ministry.

That was the "best of times"—miracles and great things were happening. Brent was also able to obtain a great job at a large company and was off to a tremendous future. After being promoted, he found himself working nights and wanted to succeed in his new role. One day, he and his best friend were out in the parking lot after work. Someone offered them some methamphetamine to boost their energy level. Unfortunately, this had been Brent's previous drug of choice, and that day was the beginning of a relapse of a vicious addiction for my son. And from that moment, his life began to disintegrate. He lost his job and just about everything that was important to him, and life for all us began to be the "worst of times."

We had tremendous support from our staff and church leaders, but as a father, I began to hear those deceptive and accusing voices enter my mind and heart. The interesting part of this story is how the deceiver did a brain switch on me and carved a deep groove in my subconscious mind and soul. Satan took the biblical words from the friend that taught me about the requirements for Levitical priesthood and those who were unable to reproduce, and then added and transferred it to the New Testament pattern of pastoral ministry in the epistles.

> *If anyone does not know how to manage his own family, how can he take care of God's church?*
>
> —1 TIMOTHY 3:5

Even though my son was well into his adult years I still felt the responsibility of a father and the condemnation of not preventing his fall and decline. It was excruciating to see my son lose his zeal and tremendous personality to very poor choices and a horrendous addiction. No one had to tell me that I had failed; I heard those words screaming from deep within. I cried, prayed, and did everything I could to help him recover from this fall. But his choices continued, and he began to run away from us and his destiny. I started to get a bitter taste of what God, our Father, feels every day when His "prodigal world" continues to wallow in their sin instead of enjoying His abundance of grace and blessings.

The seed of failure within me began to grow again, and I felt I had to bury it and move on to take care of my responsibilities. After all, where could I go, and who would understand this very complex situation? None of us fully understood the battle my son was facing, and we had very little ability or opportunity to help him rectify his poor choices and future destiny. Sin is cruel, and rebellion hardens the process. It separates us from the resources that we so desperately need. Unless you have been there, no one knows the pain of the father, the mother, or the son, when this kind of dissipation occurs. But we know there is One in Heaven, who knows and loves His children and never gives up on them. God knows their name and has engraved it on the palm of His hand.[12]

BEGINNING SEEDS OF "THE HAPPY DANCE!"

The beginning seeds for my *(Phil)"Happy Dance!"* started on one of the worst weather days in California.

We were coming home from a trip to Redding. We had just returned our son to his home after an intervention we had initiated. Brent agreed to go with us and meet with someone he had always admired. My son, an avid baseball player and card collector had always thought so highly of Albie Pearson, who had been an all-star major league baseball player. When Brent was a young child, Albie had many times stayed in our home and played a crucial role in our healing experience of not having natural children.

While we were meeting at Albie's church in southern California, our intervention plan began to unravel and come apart at the seams. And when it did, the intervention made a dramatic transition. As Albie prayed, I felt this tremendous pressure. It had built up within me and was crying out, "I can never quite measure up and do enough. I am not even able to do a successful intervention!" The seeds of inadequacy and not measuring up due to my own feelings of failure were rising up again and spilled out in a flood of tears. I thought I had been healed in these areas, but in the midst of this battle, they surfaced. Albie prayed and affirmed me, and another layer of my pain was removed. But it was not the time or cadence for *"THE Happy Dance!"*

It was during this stormy and unforgettable drive home from Redding that the clouds of blessing began to burst forth. With much pain in my heart, that was the day I asked Debby to forgive me for keeping her from having natural children of her own. My tears appeared much larger than the raindrops as this purifying process took place. Debby, a very gifted multi-tasker, listened while driving during a terrible storm. And as we prayed and cried together, the cleansing streams of Jesus' blood poured forth.

During this drive, my own tremendous standard of never being "enough" was exposed. I could never quite measure up, *be* enough, or *do* enough. I had become my own harsh taskmaster! That evening the emotional dam broke, and as I acknowledged my "Stronghold" and gave my brokenness to God, a new freedom was beginning to spring up within me. The release began, and preparation for *"THE Happy Dance"* was on the way.

I HAD BECOME MY OWN HARSH TASKMASTER!

So, we now return to that moment when Debby shared with me her Christmas request. Well, I would love to say I jumped up and began to dance and shout! But I knew in my heart that I wasn't yet ready.

I had to pull down the lingering *remnants* of my "Stronghold". And I had to no longer need to "understand" (soul). I had chosen not to let my feelings dominate, so I had buried them—and instead chose for my mind and logic to rule (soul). I needed to understand "why" and "what". "Why" God had allowed these circumstances, and "what" good had been brought by them.

I had even seen with my own eyes my wife's joy and peace on a whole different level than I had ever experienced. I wanted it, but I also wanted to really "understand" it. I discovered that my logical mind was holding me back.

I needed to be able to say and believe with full assurance the words of the Psalmist, "Praise the Lord, my soul; all my inmost being (soul and spirit), praise His Holy Name." (Psalm 103:1)

But the brain has the capacity to absorb and maintain in its memory—traumatic or erroneous perceptions—that can alter and define and even control our thoughts and actions for years, decades, and even lifetimes. Keeping us "frozen in time!"

Like Naaman in the Old Testament[13]—I had to plunge into a dirty river of past hurts, self-inflicted wounds, and false perceptions—to be totally cleansed and released from those parts of my life that had been consumed by the enemy and had affected my spirit, soul, and body. In my spirit, I was conscious of God's love and providence, but my soul had been tortured by lies, buried pain, a perversion of truth—as well as my inner critic that assumed that I needed to carry these burdens. I did not realize that I was "frozen in time!"

And as I offered all my pain to God, He began restoring my soul and healing my innermost being. I had to instruct my soul to embrace what my spirit "Knew" from listening to the Holy Spirit, my "real" Life Coach. I had to throw my arms of logic and feelings around the "Knowing" of my spirit—that the Omniscient One (All-Knowing) is also my Heavenly Father, "A good, good Father."

His plan has always been to give me the very best, and it is His perfect will for my life. My soul's understanding was limited, and I had leaned on my *own* understanding. But His plan, though not completely understood by my finite (limited) mind, was His infinite (boundless) and perfect plan for my life.

I then finally *chose* (soul) to celebrate and to rejoice in the Lord always! Then my body was able to delight in great joy because freedom had come to my spirit and soul. With deep gratitude and joy, I found myself ready to dance! I had just found my "missing piece"!

Although I had never learned to dance like David in the Bible, I unabashedly and unashamedly, "Danced before the Lord."[14] Finally, I presented my gift to Debby. But it was really a "joy unspeakable" gift to me from a "Good, Good Father." *"THE Happy Dance"* before *"The Lord of the Dance"* was an expression and an acknowledgment of God's promise—to redeem and restore all the years the enemy had attempted to sow tares (noxious poison) of his torture in my soul. I was no longer "frozen in time!"

> *So, if the Son ("The Lord of the Dance") sets you free, you will be free indeed.*
> —JOHN 8:36, Brackets Added

It's *"THE Happy Dance!"*

You probably have not had the same experience, but we have *all* had life experiences that have affected our life. If you have been "frozen in time" due to a trial or trauma as a child or adult, this can be your time to thaw out and experience His freedom and joy.

Come join us on a journey of *transformation* by moving beyond the average Christian experience. We invite you to personally find the "missing pieces" that complete the steps to your *"Happy Dance!"* We desire that when "The Lord of the Dance" inquires of you, "May I have this dance?"—you will have been *transformed* by the truths in these pages—spirit, soul, and body—and that your feet won't miss a step as you begin your triumphant *"Happy Dance!"*

"It *is* well with my soul!" Now I am *"Victorious*—spirit, soul, and body! Now that's Living!

> *"You're a good, good FATHER... it's Who You are!*
> *And I'm loved by You... it's who I am!* [15]

I am being TRANSFORMED... *By Being Set Free!*

Study Questions

1. Would you say that you are "teachable" and desire to be changed?

    ☐ Yes   OR   ☐ No

2. What areas do you desire change?

    Explain: _____

    _____

    _____

    _____

    _____

    _____

3. Look up Matthew 26:38-41. What event or circumstance caused Jesus to speak these words?

    _____

    _____

    _____

    _____

4. Have you ever been aware of your own "Spiritual Knowing"?

   ☐ Yes   OR   ☐ No

   Explain: _____

   _____

   _____

   _____

   _____

   _____

5. Have you experienced circumstances in life that were difficult to understand or endure?

   ☐ Yes   OR   ☐ No

   Explain: _____

   _____

   _____

   _____

   _____

   _____

6. Do you or have you ever had to instruct your soul to embrace what your spirit "knew"?

   ☐ Yes   OR   ☐ No

   Explain: _____

   _____

   _____

   _____

   _____

   _____

7. Have you had the opportunity for your own "Happy Dance"?

   ☐ Yes   OR   ☐ Not Yet

   If YES, explain: _____

   _____

   _____

   _____

   _____

   _____

Chapter Three
"May I Have This Dance?"

Everything goes through a period of metamorphosis—technology, trends, relationships—even stress and emotional pain go through changes. Over time, stress and pain can be alleviated or can intensify, but they will *not* remain stagnate.

METAMORPHOSIS OF PAIN

I *(Phil)* had experienced a metamorphosis of my pain. It had changed, so I did not recognize it, but it was definitely from the same root. I did not measure up to my own standard—first as a man, and then as a father. When metamorphosis occurs, the wound changes into something unrecognizable. Over time we fail to identify our wounds from their original state. This allows them to fester, causing them to deepen and become more entrenched. Anger would be a good example in this instance. If you were angry at someone, every time that you saw that person, heard that person's voice, or thought of that person—it would cause you to become angry. Over time that anger could metamorphose into bitterness. Bitterness would now become your norm, and from there, bitterness would branch out and affect your way of thinking in your daily life.

Many people, especially men, push down, ignore, and even repress their pain and its origin. Some fortify the pain with excuses and reasons. Even spiritual encounters can calcify the pain if you don't fully and *completely* deal with the root causes. They must be exposed, and then we must be willing to look them in the eye!

Healing can only begin when there is *bravery* and *honesty* and *humility*.

1. BRAVERY

You must be brave enough to face your pain—you must look at how you *have* handled it or *have not* handled it.

Phil was finishing his doctorate in psychology and needed to conduct interviews with people in different age groups. My mother *(Debby)* was spending a couple of weeks with us, and it was a perfect opportunity to interview her for the age group of over 70. We were just finishing a meal when Phil proposed one of the questions: "Do you have any regrets in your life?"

My mother was the wife of a pastor and a very strong woman. With such pain coming across her face, I couldn't imagine what regret she was experiencing. And this day, my own mother's very deep pain abruptly surfaced. Buried pain brings stress whenever something reminds you of a traumatic event or a source of pain; you feel it and then try to push it away. You think you have buried it, but it is still alive, waiting to surface at any moment.

My mother's older sister had committed suicide and left behind three young children. This much I knew. But I wasn't prepared to hear my mother say, "I was responsible for my sister's death!" You see, their father was a pastor of a church in a very small Midwest town. And the rumor mill was running overtime with details of her sister having an affair. When that news reached my mother, she immediately shared what the community was gossiping about with her father. Their father then confronted her sister, and later that day, she was discovered outside of town in her car with a self-inflicted gunshot wound. Not only did my mother feel responsible, but her siblings condemned her and blamed her, as well.

How does a teenaged young woman handle that kind of trauma? In this case, she didn't. She suppressed it, she ignored it, and she tried to outrun it. She did everything within her power to try to forget her role in this tragedy. But the only thing these actions accomplished was to change the appearance of the hurt, but the original grievance was still there.

What untold consequences did that buried pain and stress inflict upon her emotions and body all of her life? Yes, the pain had changed, but it was still alive within her soul. She was still "frozen in time!"

Phil asked the second interview question, "How did you deal with your regret?" As the pain and shame tumbled out, she expressed that she had never really talked about this tragedy with *anyone*, not even my dad—and said she wasn't sure why she was doing so today. Could it be that her Heavenly Father wanted her to be finally free and healed of this life-long burden? Now, I had a better understanding of why when her sister's husband had a mental breakdown shortly after her suicide, my mother scooped up their three children and brought them into her home and became their surrogate mother. On this day in our home, my mother finally became brave enough to come face-to-face with her pain.

2. HONESTY

The second step in the healing process is to deal honestly with the repercussions—look at your part in the pain—what you did (soul/body) with the pain, and your own reaction (soul/body) to the pain.

My mother had a "Spiritual Knowing" that God did not count this tragic event against her. The real issue was that her own soul, and the enemy of her soul, had condemned her every day since that heartbreaking event. She had to finally forgive herself and the other family members that had held her captive to her own guilt and shame.

DEAL HONESTLY WITH THE REPERCUSSIONS—LOOK AT YOUR PART IN THE PAIN—WHAT YOU DID (SOUL/BODY) WITH THE PAIN AND YOUR OWN REACTION (SOUL/BODY) TO THE PAIN.

---

3. HUMILITY

The third and final step is humility. You must be willing to humble yourself and let it all go—the pain, the refuse, and the ramifications. And say, *"Okay, Soul, let it go!"*

Your soul must come into agreement with what your spirit "Knows"—that you are forgiven and loved. And that you agree (spirit, soul, body) with God's will and plan for your life, as painful as it might have been, or still may be.

I wish that we had known about *"THE Happy Dance"* so that my mother could have identified her own "missing piece". How I wish that we had known about the steps for *"THE Happy Dance!"* the day of my mom's interview. I know my mother felt release and freedom from the guilt and condemnation, but what about the joy!

"THE LORD OF THE DANCE" ASKS, "MAY I HAVE THIS DANCE?"

Our first *"Happy Dance"* experience was at our salvation. Okay, it wasn't quite a dance yet, so let's call it the *"Happy Step!"*

My spirit recognizes that I desperately need a Savior, and then my spirit directs my soul and body to respond. At this realization, I take down all my defenses and excuses, and my heart and soul ask Jesus to enter my life—we do this with a confession of my sin and a prayer response (spirit/soul/body).

It is the first time that our spirit, soul, and body come into alignment. It's the *"Happy Step!"* I need Him, so I will respond to the Holy Spirit and "take" Jesus Christ into my life. That is just the beginning of our new life, and it is the first step in our spiritual journey. We need faith, teaching, growth, and experience to *grow* into maturity. But if I only allow Jesus into my spirit, I will remain just a "taker"—a babe in Christ.

IT IS THE FIRST TIME THAT MY SPIRIT, SOUL, AND BODY COME INTO ALIGNMENT. IT'S THE *"HAPPY STEP!"*

We can soak up head knowledge and spiritual knowledge, but unless we make room for God into our whole being—our spirit, soul, and body—we will never be everything that God had intended for us. We will continue to be vulnerable to the other members of our being (soul/body) and their desire to rule. 1. Our mind: by our logic and reasoning. 2. Our emotions: by our feelings and moods. 3. Our body: by our sensations, needs, and drives.

Victorious Christian Living necessitates that our spirit rules our being and that we require our soul and our body to become responders to our spirit that is being influenced by the Holy Spirit. When this occurs, we are not just "takers" but are "givers"—giving God access to our whole life and world. It is allowing "The Lord of the Dance" to be the Lord of our life and being willing to rejoice with His master plan.

It is not taking charge of my own life. It is not being driven by *my* needs or preferences. It is not being fearful or discouraged. It is no longer grieving over what could or should have been. I must *give* God complete access to my being and actually *want* to experience *"THE Happy Dance!"*

"THE HAPPY DANCE" CAN'T OCCUR WITH A RELUCTANT PARTNER

Synergy is the working together of two or more people, organizations, or things, especially when the *result* is greater than the sum of their individual effects or capabilities.[16] When our spirit, soul, and body come into alignment and agreement with the Holy Spirit, there is *synergy*, there is increased power, and something happens. It's *kinetic:* energy that an object or system has because it is moving.[17] Yes, it's *"THE Happy Dance!"*

"May I Have This Dance?"

You have turned my mourning into joyful dancing. You have taken away my clothes of mourning and clothed me with joy.

—PSALM 30:11, NLT

Our spirit can have a most Holy Spirit-inspired thought or "Knowing", but it is then up to our other parts—our soul and body—to agree. What if the Lord called us front and center for our *"Happy Dance"* and our emotions say, "Sounds good but I don't *feel* it yet"? Or what if our spirit and soul agree, but our body stubbornly declares, "Sounds really good, but I'm not moving—I'm staying in my chair"? *"THE Happy Dance"* can't occur with a reluctant partner. It requires the synergy of our spirit, soul, and body!

The more we filter our soul's thoughts, ideas, and even our emotions through our spirit, the more spiritually alive and mature we become. We have to rein in our soul's need to understand and allow that need to come under the influence of our spirit.

Then our soul—with its mindsets and prejudices, its logic and reasoning, its feelings and emotions—finally chooses to agree with what our Holy Spirit-inspired spirit knew all along. This is when, finally, our soul catches up with our spirit. This produces synergy—and the result is greater than the sum of our spirit or our soul's effects or capabilities.

When our soul and our body come into alignment and agreement with our Holy Spirit-infused spirit, something happens—it is kinetic, it produces motion—and the body responds. It's *"THE Happy Dance!"*

And I can finally declare: *"Now I get it, now I understand!"*

"THE Happy Dance" is almost ready to happen when I consent for my soul—my own thinking, ideas, and emotions—to come into

alignment with the Holy Spirit. But I must choose to add the final ingredient—*gratitude*. I can be obedient in my soul and body without thankfulness, but if I do, I will miss the emotion that the spirit contributes—pure *joy*! Thankfulness produces joy because gratitude dissipates doubt, cynicism, and judgments.

Gratefulness is the final surrender to acknowledging that God's will really is perfect! It recognizes that He does know what is best for me, and I choose to say, "Yes, I agree with You, God, and I'm even *grateful*!" I have just found the "missing piece!"

Our spirit must assume the position of influence over our being, and instruct and teach our soul— if we are to be Victorious!

When our soul and body stop fighting what our spirit knows to be true, we must then make the right choice. We must choose to agree and actually *celebrate* God's love, His will and His plan with a *thankful* heart. A reaction springs forth—it's *"THE Happy Dance!"*

Rejoice before you see the result or answer to your prayer. Rejoice before the victory. Thankfulness changes our soul's attitudes and thoughts. Thankfulness elevates the spirit over the soul. Thankfulness even changes the atmosphere around us. Our spirit is able to encourage, or even push our soul to be grateful. Grateful for His love, sacrifice, salvation, provision, mercy, grace, instruction, His plan, and yes—even his discipline and correction. When our rejoicing spirit urges our soul to be thankful, something happens—it's *"THE Happy Dance!"*

Our natural soul tends to concentrate on what we feel is lacking or is missing from our life. If you live any length of time on this earth, you will experience some pain, discouragement, disappointment, or depression. It happens to each of us. Since God's will is to *restore* our soul, He uses all of these components to *refine* (to remove impurities or unwanted elements)[18] our soul. In His refinement process, He restores our soul back to His original design—producing changes in us that fulfill His purpose for our life. But if you stay stuck and see the pain or the circumstances of refinement only as a difficult thing, you will never be able to see it as a blessing and experience the joy of *"THE Happy Dance!"* You will miss the joy and be left holding only your perceived "lack" or your pain.

You will be toting around complicated baggage. Your "nurse and rehearse", or your resentment will cloud your view of your world. God's holy influence will be obscured. Your wounds keep your spirit stifled, leaving your soul in charge, and "frozen in time!"

YOUR WOUNDS KEEP YOUR SPIRIT STIFLED, LEAVING YOUR SOUL IN CHARGE AND "FROZEN IN TIME!"

EXPERIENCING *"THE HAPPY DANCE!"*

Mary's world was bombarded when an angel appeared and delivered the message that she was going to have a baby. She had a question like we all do when we don't understand God's plan, and she asked, "How?" The angel explained that the Holy Spirit would come upon her, and she would conceive—the very Son of God.

> *"I am the Lord's servant," Mary responded, "May Your word to me be fulfilled."*
>
> —LUKE 1:38

At this point, Mary acquiesced to God's plan. But could she be wondering if she would lose Joseph, her own Prince Charming? The excitement of her wedding day and starting their lives together would be so different than the one that Mary had envisioned and planned. She knew there would be whispers, and accusations, and judgments. She had heard them all before—about other women. She knew no one would understand.

Mary then left town to visit her aunt Elizabeth. Elizabeth had been unable to get pregnant, but now miraculously, Elizabeth had finally conceived and was in her sixth month of pregnancy.

> *When Elizabeth heard Mary's greeting, the baby leaped in her womb, and Elizabeth was filled with the Holy Spirit. In a loud voice she exclaimed: "Blessed are you among women and blessed is the child you will bear! But why am I so favored, that the mother of my Lord should come to me? As soon as the sound of your greeting reached my ears, the baby*

> *in my womb leaped for joy. Blessed is she who has believed that the Lord would fulfill His promises to her!"*
>
> —LUKE 1:41-45

In Elizabeth's womb, her baby's spirit was responding to the Holy One, and there was kinetic energy, and her baby leaped for joy—it was *"THE Happy Dance!"*

When Elizabeth confirmed the angel's words, Mary stopped trying to figure it out on her own or to try to understand why God would do it this way. Instead, she chose to *agree* with the perfect will of God and saw it as a good thing—it was a very good thing!

> *And Mary said: "My soul glorifies the Lord and my **spirit rejoices** in God my Savior."*
>
> —LUKE 1:46-47, Emphasis Added

This verse said that her spirit *"rejoices"*. That word in the original language of the Bible means getting so *glad one jumps* in celebration; to *exult* (*boast*) because *so experientially joyful.*[19] It was *"THE Happy Dance!"*

That day Mary chose to rejoice because she knew that something more wonderful than her own plan was being accomplished—the world was getting the Savior that it so desperately needed! Her earthly pain would be worth the fulfillment of God's plan. She saw her new life as the blessing it was, and her spirit rejoiced. She understood how blessed she was. God's plan was necessary, and she didn't only adjust to His plan—Mary chose to rejoice in His plan.

THE Happy Dance

When "The Lord of the Dance," asks us to dance, we must say "Yes!"—and give up our own design, discouragement, disappointment, and despair. You can't dance holding on to baggage; we must lay it down and desire to rejoice!

As an elementary school student, I *(Debby)* remember Friday afternoons. When the teacher would say, "Class, push back your desks!" the whole room was filled with relief and excitement. It meant we could finally put away all of the tedious work of scholarly study, and now it's time to Square Dance! Yes, everyone but me. You see, I was raised in a pastor's home, and dancing was "against our religion". Every Friday that I was in elementary school—I was left sitting on the sidelines—left feeling out-of-place, awkward, like I didn't fit-in, and totally embarrassed. Finally, in about the fourth grade, a teacher must have noticed my body language and asked me to operate the record player—and yeah, I became the DJ! For the rest of my elementary education, that became my new role, and I was relieved to now not be left sitting all alone at my desk.

You can only imagine how meaningful *"THE Happy Dance"* is to me. When the Holy Spirit hit my own spirit on Ferguson Road, it changed my soul's mindset forever. That day Jesus the Bridegroom, "The Lord of the Dance," was saying to this bride, *"May I have this dance?"* My answer to Him was, "I don't know how to dance!" But God is patient, and His response to me was, *"Let **Me** teach you to dance!"*

He taught me that day like He had taught Mary, to not just acquiesce to God's plan for my life. To not simply comply with lingering reservations, but to actually celebrate and rejoice in His plan. I don't know if the angels in heaven were playing the old-fashioned turntable that day, but I know they were rejoicing when

"May I Have This Dance?"

I got up from observing from the sidelines of life. I said "Yes!" to Jesus and was finally able to learn the most important dance of all—"*THE Happy Dance*" of rejoicing and celebrating God!

I can finally say that I have learned not to just acquiesce to God's plan. I have learned to rejoice and dance! Paul knew the importance and instructed, "Rejoice in the Lord always. I will say it again: Rejoice!" (Philippians 4:4)

I CAN FINALLY SAY THAT I HAVE LEARNED NOT TO JUST ACQUIESCE TO GOD'S PLAN. I HAVE LEARNED TO REJOICE AND DANCE!

After God parted the Red Sea for the Israelites to escape from their slavery in Egypt, the people of Israel put their trust in God—they were in awe of Him and agreed with His plan.

And then Miriam, sister of Moses, picked up her tambourine, and in celebration, sang and danced before the Lord.[20] She was rejoicing in her God and His provision and plan. It was *"THE Happy Dance!"*

The Ark of the Covenant was extraordinary because it represented the "Presence of God." After years of preparation, it was finally time to bring the Ark of the Covenant home to a proper place of honor. God had placed the desire in David's spirit, it became his heart and soul's passion, and finally, the day had come. His spirit, soul, and body were aligned, and it was time for *"THE Happy Dance!"*

THE Happy Dance

> *As the ark of the covenant of the Lord was entering the City of David, Michal daughter of Saul watched from a window. And when she saw King David **dancing** and **celebrating**, she despised him in her heart.*
>
> —1 CHRONICLES 15:29, Emphasis Added

It was a dance of celebration—but how tragic that David's own wife could not share in this triumphant and joyful experience with her husband. He was celebrating and was free in spirit, soul, and body—but she could not connect with the celebration. Instead, she remained bound by her judging and cynical soul and by her own emotions. I wonder what had happened in Michal's life that kept her "frozen in time!"

It *is* possible to have the kinetic energy of merging spirit, soul, and body without actually kicking up your heels, but why would you refrain? It is allowing the Holy Spirit full reign and control of your being. And the effect is feeling alive in your spirit and being at peace in your soul, which produces positive energy into your body. The result is pure joy!

If I don't have peace and joy in my daily life, I do a mental inventory and ask myself, "What am I feeling and who (spirit, soul, or body) is in charge of my being right now?" This question provides me the opportunity to ask the Holy Spirit to move into the situation so that my emotions and desires or logic do not drive me.

William Law was a seventeenth-century theologian who championed the devout and holy life. "Would you know who is the greatest saint in the world? It is not he who prays most or fasts most; it is not he who gives most alms or is most eminent for temperance, chastity, or justice; but it is he who is always thankful to

God, who wills everything that God wills, who receives everything as an instance of God's goodness and has a heart always ready to praise God for it." —*William Law*

Now my spirit, soul, and body—in perfect synergy—rejoice and declare:

> *"You're a good, good Father... it's Who You are!*
> *And I'm loved by You... it's who I am!*
> *You are perfect in all of Your ways to us (ME)!"*[21]

I want to make "The Lord of the Dance" the Lord of my life! This is "Living!" I am "*Victorious*"—in my spirit, my soul, and my body! And with God's help, I won't settle for anything less!

I am being TRANSFORMED...
By Being Brave!
By Being Honest!
By Being Humble!
By Being Grateful!

Study Questions

1. Have you discovered the remnants of past pain that you haven't fully dealt with or received healing?

   ☐ Yes OR ☐ No

   Explain: _____
   _____
   _____
   _____

2. Did you experience a metamorphosis of your pain?

   ☐ Yes OR ☐ No

3. Could you trace it to another scenario, yet see that it is the same root?

   ☐ Yes OR ☐ No

   Explain: _____
   _____
   _____
   _____

4. Review the three "Steps to Healing" on Pages 46-49. Are you brave enough to start the process?

   ☐ Yes OR ☐ No

   Explain: _____

   _____

   _____

   _____

   _____

   _____

5. Have you made room for God in your spirit, soul, and body?

   ☐ Yes OR ☐ No

6. Do you find it easy to process your thoughts through your spirit?

   ☐ Yes OR ☐ No

7. Have you experienced your own "Happy Dance?"

   ☐ Yes OR ☐ Not Yet

   Explain: _____

   _____

   _____

   _____

   _____

   _____

Chapter Four

Are You Out of Your Mind?

Then God said, "Let Us make mankind in Our image, in Our likeness."

—GENESIS 1:26

When Adam and Eve were created by God, they were perfect—perfect in every way! Can you imagine that feeling?"

And they felt no shame.

—GENESIS 2:25

Can you picture the freedom and confidence that Adam and Eve enjoyed? Can you envision living without the negative emotions of imperfection, unworthiness, or regret? Can you imagine not having to battle against the negative triad of fear, shame, and pain? Can you imagine how being free from this negativity would impact our relationship with God and each other?

How long did this condition of perfection, peace, and tranquility last? We don't know how long exactly, but this perfect condition was referenced in the final verses of chapter two of Genesis, and by the beginning of chapter three man's destiny was forever changed!

I don't believe Eve's thinking that day was to remove God from her life. But she coveted that ability to "be like God"—she wanted to know and decide what is right for "me". How many of us think at times that things would be so much more efficient and run more smoothly if I knew all that God knows? Perfect—that's how things would be if I were in charge!

Eve's decision was based in selfishness—she chose to go her own way, rather than be obedient to God. That day "self" was exalted above God. With Eve's decision to go against God, her eyes were opened just like her enemy had predicted, but what she saw was not perfection, as she had presumed.

Yes, she had become like God in the area of recognizing what is right and wrong. And what Eve saw was so appalling that it had to be covered and hidden. Now she felt shame for the first time. Eve saw her imperfection, and her own self-centeredness caused it. That day our human soul became influenced by "self".

Previously we wrote about the life-changing, rainy and long trip home from Redding. That day my wife said, "I think your own standards for you are even higher than God's! I think that you can never measure up to your own expectations. Enough never seems to be enough! You are a harsh taskmaster! You have had a good life; you have a master's Degree and two Doctoral Degrees, is that enough?" Quite frankly, in my natural self, I would say "no." Because most humans live with a fear of never having enough, never doing enough, and never being enough.

Are You Out of Your Mind?

Housed within our human soul is our "mind". And it was Eve's mind that led her down a path of destruction and separation from God. Our redeemed human spirit "Knows", but our human mind wants to "understand" and "decide". Because after sin entered the world, man became "self" focused!

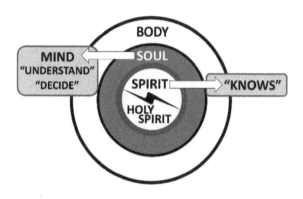

"HAVE YOU LOST YOUR MIND?"

Paul, the Apostle, was a man who could be described as a tentmaker, preacher, apostle, teacher, psychologist, and philosopher. By the inspiration of the Holy Spirit, Paul wrote and taught specific principles that have to do with our thinking, our mindset, and the vital importance of renewing the mind. He taught us that we could have the mind of Christ,[22] a mind of peace.[23] But Paul also taught that our minds could be our own worst enemy and hostile to God.[24] The mind can either be a powerful instrument of peace or a defiant insurgent of chaos and unbelief.

When someone does something harmful to themselves or others, and it is out of character, impulsive, or under the influence of other external factors—a friend might say to them, "Have you lost your mind?" Or "Are you crazy?" Or they might say, "What were you thinking?" They are describing the "soul that is out of control."

That person is giving something in exchange for their soul. What was man thinking when he began to serve the creature rather than the Creator?[25] It does not make sense, but it happens far too often.

Jesus stated it so succinctly,

*What would it profit a man if he gained the whole world, but lost his **soul** or what could a man give in exchange for his **soul**?*

—MATTHEW 16:26, Emphasis Added

It is interesting to observe in the American culture a paradigm shift. Thinking has been replaced by a new and different pattern—from pneuma (spirit) to psyche (mind). Our culture has emphasized the rational side of man at the cost of losing the influence of our Creator. The psychology of understanding the mind of man has proliferated, and the study of the spirit (knowing God) has declined.

In the last decade alone, we have seen a heavy emphasis on "Mindfulness" and a renewed interest in Buddhism. Mindfulness emphasizes the importance of focusing on the present moment, and as your thoughts rush through your mind, you are to view them without judgment. Mindfulness contrasts with a contemplative meditation that has been the practice of Christians throughout history.

I rejoice in following Your statutes as one rejoices in great riches. I meditate on Your precepts and consider Your ways.

—PSALM 119:15

Instead of focusing upon the spirit's "Knowing" God, the focus is now on the soul's mind "understanding" your own thoughts without judgment. We are in danger of losing our minds to ourselves and totally missing the mind of God that brings freedom.

WE ARE IN DANGER OF LOSING OUR MINDS TO OURSELVES AND TOTALLY MISSING THE MIND OF GOD THAT BRINGS FREEDOM.

STEPS TO UNDERSTANDING

When we are born, our mind has innate and intuitive knowledge—meaning we don't have to learn it. Then as we mature, our mind's awareness is expanded as new knowledge is acquired through experience that comes to us from all directions. As Christians, we should desire a propensity to develop a discerning mind—a mind that is under God's holy influence. We need God's instruction and God's new knowledge.

All new knowledge is imparted through the mind. But before new knowledge can be life-changing, it passes through four different steps. The first step is to "Comprehend" this knowledge; you have to understand and grasp its meaning. You have to be able to explain it to yourself.[26]

And the second step is you must "Apprehend", which is to *really* understand and grasp the meaning and see the importance or significance of this new knowledge.[27]

Then the third step is we must "Embrace" and fervently agree with this new knowledge—it must be taken as settled.[28]

But before this new knowledge can be beneficial or life-changing, the fourth step is necessary. We must "Apply" and put into practice[29] *new* knowledge—otherwise, it just remains *head* knowledge.

The understanding of this new knowledge can come from either God (to our spirit), or from our flawed and imperfect mind (soul), which the devil can influence. This understanding can be God-inspired wisdom, or it can be simply human wisdom. It must be tested by the Holy Spirit.

I *(Debby)* have a very good friend, and she has the most engaging way of making you feel valued—she asks a lot of questions. Not as a busy body but in a genuinely loving and affectionate manner. And because she is also so teachable, whenever I receive a call from her and it begins with, "So, Debby..." I get excited in my spirit. She is so spiritually hungry that I know God has been stirring something deep within her, and she wants new insight, clarification, or confirmation. Such a call came early one summer. Her friend had just gone to her secular counselor, and they instructed that her difficult in-laws were not her concern—they were her husband's. She didn't have to do anything in their relationship! She didn't have to be with them if she didn't want to be—she was free!

During this phone call my friend asked, "Debby, our in-laws are just alike. Does that apply to me?" My friend had just looked at her calendar and realized that her family had previously made out-of-town plans—and even a vacation—to be with her in-laws every weekend for the next six weeks! My reply to her was, "What do you think?" She said, "It sounds so good... but..." She was saying that it sounded so good to her soul because her mind agreed with it, but her own spirit was sensing that maybe this was man's wisdom and not God's wisdom.

I replied, "You can do whatever you want, it is your decision. People tell us to build up walls of protection around us, and they call them boundaries. But God tells us to pull down our walls and reach out to them in love. What if God has provided you with a mission field this summer? What if God wants to use you to demonstrate what God's love looks like?"

At the end of six weeks, I received a call from my friend. She began with, "You won't believe it... oh yes, you will—I've been on a mission field!" My friend went on to relay how God had used her to love—with attitude, words, and actions. She had two significant spiritual encounters and felt so blessed and honored to be used by God to bring faith and insight. The morning before our phone conversation, my friend was getting ready and was overcome with the joy of having been used by God. She stated, "I was so joyful I was literally jumping up and down!" I said, "Did you just say that you were jumping up and down with joy? Oh, that's *"THE Happy Dance!"* My friend had rejected the temptation to settle for man's understanding and wisdom. She made herself available to be used by God. She placed others above her own hurt feelings and needs. And "The Lord of the Dance" asked, *"May I have this Dance?"*

WE ARE OUR "MIND!"

From conception, we are "fearfully and wonderfully made".[30] We are influenced by what we have learned. As our mind begins to associate certain messages in our surroundings, a pathway within the brain is formed. Even before a child is born, these pathways of electrochemical messages between neurons are being formed within the brain. The more often a pathway is used, it becomes more sensitive and developed, and then becomes routine. That new pathway becomes stronger the more it is used, which causes new long-term connections and memories. As these pathways continue to develop, the combined collection of used pathways forms a map of how we think, how we reason, and then how we remember.

We are our "mind!" It's as simple as that—what we think about or even what we try to push *out* of our mind—dictates who we become. Now for the good news, even good habits are just that—habits. The more we practice good habits, the more they become second nature—and eventually a lifestyle.

Our mind is so powerful because, as an individual, it houses our distinctive and unique thoughts. All our feelings, emotions, memories, perceptions, attitudes, and beliefs become the *filter* through which we live every moment of our life. Every thought and each *new* experience pass through that filter. And that filter becomes our *"mindset"*—it is our point of reference, our reality, and everything flows through it.

ALL OUR FEELINGS, EMOTIONS, MEMORIES, PERCEPTIONS, ATTITUDES, AND OUR BELIEFS BECOME THE *FILTER* THROUGH WHICH WE LIVE EVERY MOMENT OF OUR LIFE.

Man's logic and audacity demand fairness. When we were moving into a brand-new home, our five-year-old and only child said, "Why do you guys get the biggest bedroom?"

Eve was saying it's "not fair" that I can't eat the most appealing fruit in the garden! That's not fair! And we also crave for everything to be "just". If I do "this", the result will always be "that". But God's Word declares,

He causes His sun to rise on the evil and the good and sends rain on the righteous and the unrighteous.

—MATTHEW 5:45

We cry out, "But that's not fair!"

CINDERELLA

I *(Debby)* want to be "Cinderella" and live happily ever after! I had a *"mindset"* that I deserved happiness, and it was up to God and me to make that happen.

I will never forget the afternoon that we received a phone call from our medical doctor that would change our lives forever. He had terrible news for us—"You will never be able to have your own natural children. It is so conclusive; don't even waste your money or go on the emotional roller coaster of fertility procedures. There is medically nothing that we can do. If you want children, I recommend that you look into adoption."

All of the emotions of our being were screaming—unbelief, sadness, anger, fear, and tremendous grief—all of the emotions that you suffer with a significant loss. And of course, my best friend had just found out she was going to have a baby. Life seemed so unfair!

ALL OF THE EMOTIONS OF OUR BEING WERE SCREAMING—UNBELIEF, SADNESS, ANGER, FEAR, AND TREMENDOUS GRIEF—ALL OF THE EMOTIONS THAT YOU SUFFER WITH A SIGNIFICANT LOSS.

Being so young and filled with so many hopes and dreams, this news seemed more than we could bear. But somehow, we made our way to talk with an adoption worker. She was able to articulate our pain. The reason we were feeling so much grief and the tremendous sense of loss— is that this pain is like losing all your children in a car accident. It is the death of all your unborn children. We would look at each other and say, "Is this really happening to us?"

We didn't have to grieve too long before we had a phone call. I had been teaching the fourth grade, and on the last day of school, I stopped by Phil's office on my way home. Phil was on the pastoral staff of a church, and he unexpectedly received a phone call. Phil looked up from the phone call, placed his hand over the receiver, and asked me, "Do you want to adopt a baby—like right now?" The caller was asking if he knew of anyone who would like to adopt a baby because the couple planning to adopt could not do so, and that baby would be born in just a matter of days.

Phil said that *we* would take the baby, and before we knew it, we had a 5-day old baby in our home! Brian Paul came to us so quickly that we had nothing prepared for his arrival—no nursery, no crib, not one adorable thing! Phil was a youth pastor and the day that we brought Brian home from the hospital, our apartment was filled with students to welcome him to his new home, family, and youth group. We found a crib, and the church gave a baby shower, now our new baby had blankets, layettes, and a new outfit to wear every day of his young life! We would just look at him and say, "Is this really happening to us?" We were so thrilled to have a baby in our home that the pain of barrenness was almost lessening its grip.

Five months later, we received another phone call that would change our lives again. It was a call from our adoption worker. We were excitedly waiting to hear the good news that the adoption was just about final. We were totally unprepared to hear her say to us that day, "I'm really sorry. I have some very disappointing news for you. Brian's mother has changed her mind about the adoption. She wants him back!" The mother was a recovering drug addict and the biological father had just died of an overdose of drugs. She was grieving his death and now wanted the baby. Again, we found ourselves saying, "Is this really happening to us?"

Once again, in a short amount of time, our lives were filled with more pain than we thought that we could endure. With our attorney present, we met with the natural mother, and then Phil and I agonized and prayed about what we should do. Our attorney was prepared to go to court to battle to keep our son. Phil and I tried to put ourselves in this young woman's shoes, and we felt tremendous compassion for her—she had made a decision, and now she had a change of mind.

But Phil and I were so bonded with this child! We had let him into every square inch of our hearts, and the thought of giving him up was so painful. We prayed, and we both knew what we were supposed to do. We knew we had to respond to her the way we would have wanted someone to respond to us. God gave Phil and me a measure of peace that He would be with us, but I will never forget the ache in our hearts the day we packed Brian's things, kissed him for the last time, and closed the door to the nursery. There was now pain on top of pain.

After having Brian ripped from our arms and hearts, it was only through God's grace that we made it through that difficult time. It seemed as though the pain would never end in our life. And then another phone call came! This one was from my father, asking the most unbelievable question, "Do you want to adopt a baby?" My first reaction was, "No way!" And I responded, "I don't want to

THE Happy Dance

go through that again!" Then my dad said, "Well, don't decide so quickly. Think about it before you say 'no'. Your mom and I are very excited!"

And again, before we knew it, we were on our way to the hospital to pick up "our" baby! This time though, I had so many apprehensions. I remember thinking "Why is this day filled with so many mixed emotions? Why am I fighting back tears of grief and tears of joy all at the same time? Why do I have such excitement and anticipation and at the same time have fear and doubt? Will this mother change her mind? Will I be able to love another baby? I still feel so much hurt; will I be able to do the right things? Can I really allow myself to get excited? Can I hope that this baby is really 'ours'? How can I keep from loving too much so that I won't get hurt again? Why do I feel so blessed by God but wonder where He has been? What's wrong with me? Why can't I make all of my emotions line up and be congruent with this blessed event?" Even the warmth and comfort coming from the car's heating system seemed to be in stark contrast with the damp fog hovering over the ground outside. My family was talking as we drove along, but I was in deep contemplation. "Will this be another disappointment? I dare not get my hopes up too much because I'm not sure if I can handle the hurt if this doesn't work out."

Growing up in America we have a sense that we are entitled to a great life, and all our dreams and wishes should come true. We expect them to happen either by simply being handed to us on a silver platter or by our own hard work. How do we handle life when everything doesn't evolve according to our secret dreams? When the doctor told us that we would not have our own natural children, I stiffened with resentment and said, "Why not!"

GROWING UP IN AMERICA WE HAVE A SENSE THAT WE ARE ENTITLED TO A GREAT LIFE, AND ALL OF OUR DREAMS AND WISHES SHOULD COME TRUE!

When we returned Brian, the baby that we were adopting, back to his natural mother, I also stiffened with hurt. And once again, I was stiffening with fear as we were finding ourselves in another difficult situation in trying to finalize the adoption of our son, Brent Phillip. For two years, we had several threats of this child also being removed from our home. It seemed like a bad dream, but we just took each day as it came. We had tremendous fear and apprehension.

I was so young, spiritually and physically, that I didn't have any idea how all of the previous years' events were taking such a toll on my life. One day a Godly man walked into our lives, sent by the Lord! Albie Pearson took one look at me, and it seemed he could see directly into my soul. God used this man to reveal knowledge that was impossible for him to know. Through the Holy Spirit, Albie was given revelation and he was overwhelmed by my grief. He just held my hands and wept for all of the pain that I was carrying.

He was so gentle. Yet the next words that Albie spoke to me were piercing, "Debby, you must forgive God!"

These words were a foreign idea to me because I knew better than to ever blame God—after all, the painful events of the last years were not His fault but were part of living in a fallen world. But then, as I examined the past and present situations, I realized I *did* blame God, only in a different way. Why didn't He *make* my life perfect, the way that I had planned? I knew God could do anything because I had experienced a miraculous healing from a neck injury. I knew God had tremendous power, so why didn't He give us our natural children? Why didn't He let us keep Brian? Why were we even having difficulties in adopting Brent? Why, Lord, why? Just then, I knew that I did need to forgive God. Forgive Him for not making my life perfect, just the way I *wanted* it to be.

You see, up until this time, I had lived my life with hardly any pain. I had wonderful Christian parents, attended a great church, and had a very positive experience as a P.K. (Pastor's Kid). In school, I was very active, made good grades, and had a lot of friends. I did suffer the usual pain of being a teenager and trying to find myself, but nothing that I couldn't deal with or fix.

I planned to marry a wonderful and loving husband, and I did. I did *not* plan on marrying a pastor or a life of ministry, but I was fixing that. We planned on having 2 or 3 children, but I could *not* fix that. God could, but He *chose* not to! Now I was faced with, "Do I want to forgive God for that? Do I really want to forgive Him for allowing all of the pain of that experience as well as the unsuccessful adoption?" I knew there were only two choices—continue to live in pain and become embittered or forgive. I had to forgive my God before I could trust Him with my whole life.

This was my first experience of becoming "poor in spirit".[31] Being poor in spirit was realizing my own spiritual poverty and seeing my tremendous need for God. I could not make it on my own! I could not handle this life without God helping me! How I needed some relief from the pain and heavy load that I was carrying. Yes, God was there giving me strength for every day, easing pain and sorrow, but I pushed down most of my honest emotions inside. These emotions were so raw and unbecoming that I really did not want to face them. But this night I came face-to-face with all of them!

THIS WAS MY FIRST EXPERIENCE OF BECOMING *"POOR IN SPIRIT"*, WHICH IS REALIZING MY OWN SPIRITUAL POVERTY AND SEEING MY TREMENDOUS NEED FOR GOD.

This night I began to pray, "God, will you still love me if I am perfectly honest with you? Well, here goes! I resent how so many other women can have children so easily! I deeply resent women being able to conceive and then deciding abortion is a better alternative for them. That seems so unfair! God, I know you created the heavens and the universe. You have healing power in Your hand, so why don't you grant me my heart's desire! My husband is such a wonderful man; why does he have to bear the pain, shame, and guilt of not being able to father natural children? God, why do You allow his pain? Yes, God, I do resent You for not making our lives perfect and not giving us our miracle! Yes, God, I do resent that You could have changed the mind of our little Brian's mother, and You could have kept us from that pain! Yes, God —You could move Your little finger and change all these circumstances. Why are You *choosing* not to move on our behalf?"

As the tears of pain and raw emotion, coupled with the tears of sincere honesty, were flowing down my face, I had just released a heavy burden! *Honesty and trust go hand in hand.* But I had been trying to trust God without being honest with Him or myself. But now, in my honesty with God, there came such love and tenderness from God. I wasn't expecting the gentleness and understanding that I felt emanating from the heart of God. He wasn't shocked or disappointed with me; He was only caring and compassionate.

Being honest with God was extremely difficult. But this next step that I needed to take was going to be just as difficult. Who was I to "forgive" the Lord? I could hardly form the words as I said, "Lord, I forgive You for not fixing everything the way I thought you should have. I forgive You!" Once again, God didn't strike me dead. The heavy load of resentments toward God and the circumstances of my life were finally off of me! As I gave to God all of my hurt, disappointment, and pain that night, I could sense a peace sweep over me. I didn't have to stay in bondage to my emotions or my pain. God was big enough to take them from me!

The last step that I needed to take was to declare, "Lord, I trust You with my whole life! I trust you with my pain. I trust You with my future. I trust You with my husband. I even trust You with Brent—he's Yours. If You want us to have him, I'll trust You. If You allow him to be taken from us, I'll trust You. If we never have natural children, I'll trust You! God, you say in Your Word that You are working everything for our good. I can't possibly see what good can come out of all this, but I will trust You to bring good."

One of the original words for trust in the Bible paints a picture of feeling safe or being free from worries. Throughout the Bible, God revealed His name to Moses and others. In each of their struggles, God displayed that He would be everything that they would need.

The name of the Lord is a strong fortress; the godly run to Him and are safe.

—PROVERBS 18:10 NLT

I didn't realize it that night, but I was putting God to the test. If He could bring good out of this mess, I really could trust Him with my whole life. My experience with the Lord that night was really the foundation of my spiritual awakening with Him. It was a spiritual landmark. Trusting God is the liberating power *to be able* to walk in obedience to Him and His Word. If we do not trust God completely, we will walk in our own ways and understanding. We will allow the circumstances around us to loom larger than life and more prominent than our faith in God. This prevents us from seeing past the circumstances and keeps us from seeing God and His goodness. We will be consumed with our problems and difficulties, and they will overwhelm us.

If we choose to trust God completely, we will begin to look for good. God has proven Himself faithful to me! His good has come out of that most challenging time of my life. As Phil and I began to trust God on a deeper level, we grew so much closer to each other as a couple. Through these experiences, our love for each other has deepened as the Lord has knit our hearts in love. We truly are one of the happiest couples that I know! Instead of the problems that we experienced the first years of our marriage driving us apart, they cemented us together. God made us "one". That is truly the "good" work of the Lord!

We must build a "Trust Account" with God. One of the tools we have used to build our trust account is looking for the goodness of God. His goodness is always there, but every day we need to intentionally look for it. There are specific Names of God that are memorial stones of His love, care, and provision. We have found that reflecting on and applying these Names of God helps us focus our attention on His presence, goodness, and promises. He is faithful and trustworthy.

"I Am"	
Exodus 3:14; 6:2-4; 34:5-7; Psalm 102	His goodness: His ability to be everything that we need.
El Shaddai—The All Sufficient One	
Genesis 17:1-3; 35:11; 48:3; 49:25; Psalm 90:2	His goodness: The Lord is always more than enough.
El Olam—The Everlasting God	
Genesis 21:33; Psalm 90:12; Isaiah 40:28	His goodness: His timelessness makes it possible to heal and set us free when we are "frozen in time".
Jehovah-jireh—The Lord will Provide	
Genesis 22:13-14; Psalm 23	His goodness: The Lord provides more than we could ever imagine.
Jehovahrophe (rapha) —The Lord Who Heals	
Exodus 15:25-27; Psalm 103:3; 147:3	His goodness: The Lord will heal us—spirit, soul, and body.
Jehovahshalom—The Lord is Peace	
Numbers 6:22-27; Judges 6:22-24; Isaiah 9:6	His goodness: The Lord brings peace in our chaotic world.
Jehovah-rohi (raah) —The Lord is My Shepherd	
Psalm 23; Isaiah 53:6	His goodness: The Lord leads, directs, protects, provides, and cares for His people.

"THE Happy Dance" is a visual demonstration of our trust in God.

I am being TRANSFORMED... By Learning to Trust God!

Study Questions

1. Has shame or guilt ever kept you silent or stagnant instead of moving forward?

   ☐ Yes OR ☐ No

   Explain: _____

   _____

   _____

   _____

2. If you could shake free of the negative emotions of imperfection, unworthiness or regret, how would this impact your relationship with God and all of the other people in your life?

   Explain: _____

   _____

   _____

   _____

   _____

   _____

3. Name an area in your life where you have wanted to "take charge!"

   Explain: _____

   _____

   _____

   _____

   _____

4. Have you ever had difficulty trying to "understand" why GOD did not move on your behalf?

   ☐ Yes   OR   ☐ No

   Explain: _____

   _____

   _____

   _____

   _____

5. We are our "mind"! Are you more prone to:

   ☐ Dwell on things   OR   ☐ Do you try to find relief by pushing thoughts out of your mind?

   Explain: _____

   _____

   _____

   _____

   _____

Chapter Five

Pull It Down!

The day when I *(Debby)* gave God all my emotional pain, He began a new work in me. But what I didn't understand at that time is that my "mindset" had been formed at a very young age. My "mindset" became the filter and point of reference for my life. It not only dictated my viewpoint and perspective, but it infringed on my relationship with God. My "mindset" demanded my standard of perfection and happiness.

MINDSET

A "mindset" comes from an inner insight, which is then revealed in a corresponding outward behavior. It is using acquired reasoned *knowledge* that is mixed with *emotion* which forms an *opinion*—and then the opinion evolves into an *action*.[32] It is where we direct our mind toward a thing, and then we seek after or strive for it[33]—whether it's material, or peace, or a reward.

Our enemy, the devil, employed his most used tactic against me, as he had used on the first woman, Eve. He loves to reveal something that we consider we lack. And just as he revealed to Eve her lack of knowledge, he revealed to me my lack of family. What I was lacking was apparent to me as I looked around at my peers. Eve's lack was even more apparent because she had a personal relationship and had conversations with God, where He revealed His knowledge to her.

Yes, the devil loves to point out our perceived hurts, lacks, needs, or desires—even some legitimate ones. But then the devil gives his *false* opinions about them which influence our "mindset." If we buy into the devil's manipulation, a "Stronghold" can be built in our mind.

"STRONGHOLD"

A "Stronghold" is a place where we feel *"incomplete"* or *"driven"* and it takes over our *"mindset"*. The "Stronghold" influences our thinking, our opinions, and our actions. A "Stronghold" is destructive—spiritually, and even physically!

A "STRONGHOLD" IS A PLACE WHERE WE FEEL "INCOMPLETE" OR "DRIVEN" AND IT TAKES OVER OUR "MINDSET."

"Strongholds" have a military connotation—imagine a fortified and strong-walled fortress. It is a heavily fortified containment of a *false* argument, presented by the devil or our own faulty thinking, in which a person seeks shelter—running to a safe place to escape reality."[34]

David Wilkerson, the founder of "Teen Challenge," a Christian-based addiction treatment program, described it this way:

"Most of us think of Strongholds as bondages or sexual trespasses, drug addictions and alcoholism—outward sins we put on the top of our worst sins list. But Paul is referring to something much worse than our human measuring of sins. A Stronghold is holding firmly to an argument. A Stronghold is an accusation planted firmly in your mind by Satan to establish lies, falsehoods, and misconceptions, especially about the character of God."[35]

And that "Stronghold" affects our emotions, resulting in detrimental feelings of fear, anger, resentment, jealousy, pride, sadness, self-pity, and all the other "self" words. With our soul's emotions now in play, our "Stronghold" becomes even *more* fortified.

The product of these negative emotions then manifest in our outward behavior—workaholic, controlling, driven, depression, or addictions to distract us or to make us feel better (alcohol, drugs, pornography, food, overeating, anorexia/bulimia, gambling, shopping/spending, hobby, or electronic devices). These look like the "Strongholds", but they are the result of the *false* argument presented by the devil himself when he magnifies and lies about our hurt, lack, need, or desire.

If you were to talk with a drug addict about "Strongholds", they would point to their addiction. It seems so apparent because the addiction has destroyed relationships, a career, and their hope of a fulfilling future. We were having a conversation with an addict when their "Stronghold" was exposed. It was so obvious and so painful that we waited for a more appropriate time to really deal with it. A couple of days passed, and we had the opportunity to share the identity of their "Stronghold"—it wasn't their addiction; it was a deep root of hurt within their soul. At that point, they responded with intense emotion and then complete denial.

A few days later they were in a teaching setting with us, and I didn't know how they would receive this lesson. Because the Lord had ordained this time together, the lesson for the day was "Strongholds". During this session, they had a most enlightened contribution. They offered, "You must include that you will defend your own "Stronghold"—just like I did mine!"

In looking back at my own "Stronghold", I had done the same thing! My "mindset" of the expectation of perfection and happiness had become a "Stronghold" of my life. Since it started at a young age, my mindset had formed a well-used pathway in my brain. A "Stronghold" was formed. The pathway was so worn that it became automatic. When my "Stronghold" was first identified, I also said, "That's not possible, I would never hold anything against God—He's perfect!" I had to withdraw my defense of my "Stronghold", and that day my "Stronghold" was identified and pulled down. God began the process of healing my hurt and pain. The devil's lies were exposed—God was *not* withholding His love from me! And I was set free from the past expectations as I began to trust God. With that experience, my "mindset" and "Stronghold" were identified and pulled down. My soul became *Victorious*! I was no longer "frozen in time!"

When Jesus faced the devil in the wilderness, He was *Victorious*! But the devil did not give up—he was willing to wait—even for Jesus!

When the devil had finished all this tempting, he left Him (Jesus) until an opportune time."

—LUKE 4:13, Brackets Added

Pull It Down!

WHEN JESUS FACED THE DEVIL IN THE WILDERNESS, HE WAS *VICTORIOUS!* BUT THE DEVIL DID NOT GIVE UP—HE WAS WILLING TO WAIT—EVEN FOR JESUS!

Through the years, the devil has also tempted me to succumb to his ploys, at a more "opportune time". The devil is prowling around, looking for just the right moment to pounce. So, now is the time for spiritual warfare to *begin*—in order to remain *Victorious*!

SPIRITUAL WARFARE

*Be strong in the Lord and in His mighty power. Put on all of God's armor so that you will be able to stand firm against all **strategies** of the devil. For we are not fighting against flesh-and-blood enemies, but against evil rulers and authorities of the unseen world, against mighty powers in this dark world, and against evil spirits in the heavenly places.*

—EPHESIANS 6:12, NLT, Emphasis Added

To build the foundation of our "Stronghold", the devil's strategy is to influence our thinking, in the same way, he tried to tempt Jesus in the wilderness. Satan begins by pointing to and emphasizing a hurt, a lack, a need, or a desire. The devil tries to instill hopelessness so that we will listen to his false arguments and become driven by our old "mindset".

Let's unmask the devil's tactics! In summary, it begins with lies presented by the devil, sometimes even using truths associated with hurts. The devil will then proceed to put his own interpretation and spin on it—which then *becomes* a lie. And when we listen to that argument and believe it, it then touches our emotions and we agree and accept it as truth. It becomes our opinion and then our mindset. This mindset is a *"Stronghold"*—and then we cannot help but to react from that *"Stronghold"* with our thoughts and actions!

The areas the devil has used to influence our thinking may result in "Strongholds" of Shame, Rejection, Anxiety, Fear, Need for Approval, People-Pleasing, Repression of Deep Hurt, Need for Perfection, Envy, Can't Measure-Up, Lack of Acceptance, Hopelessness, Helplessness, Never Satisfied, Feeling De-Valued, Feeling Insignificant, Unforgiveness, Bitterness, Self-Pity, Self-Hatred, and Rebellion.

> What makes you angry—what is behind the anger?
> *That* is the "Stronghold"!

> What makes you sad—what is behind the sadness?
> *That* is the "Stronghold"!

> What makes you fearful—what is behind the fear?
> *That* is the "Stronghold"!

It is imperative to identify your own "Stronghold" because if you don't identify your "Strongholds", they will never come down. Why is it so much easier to see someone else's "Stronghold"? I caution you not to look at the list and point to another's place of struggle. But with intense prayer and self-examination—use this list to allow the Holy Spirit to help identify your own "Stronghold".

Even though Jesus Christ was tempted, He walked away *Victorious!* He becomes our example of standing and fighting our enemy, the devil.

> *For though we live in the world, we do not wage war as the world does. The weapons we fight with are not the weapons of the world. On the contrary, they have divine power to demolish* **strongholds**.
> —2 CORINTHIANS 10:3-4, Emphasis Added

Jesus Christ gives us the power to demolish our "Strongholds." Paul goes on to tell us *how* to do it! "We *demolish…*" The word for "demolish" in the Greek language that the New Testament was originally written, means that we are to take it down *"for oneself."*[36] *We* are to forcibly yank it down! It is destroyed, and nothing is left standing or even in good working order. It has become rubble heaped on the ground! We have determined that our own "Stronghold" must come down!

> *We demolish arguments and every* **pretension** *that sets itself up against the* **knowledge** *of God…*
> —2 CORINTHIANS 10:5, Emphasis Added

Pretension is a calculated argument, *reaching a personal opinion.*[37] It is our own "mindset!" And it must be demolished if it conflicts with what we know to be Truth, that which we "Know" in our spirit and have experienced by our relationship with God. For instance, the "mindset" that feels we can never measure-up must be demolished because it is against what God has spoken to us—we are created in His image. God says we are forgiven and loved!

> *... and we take captive every thought to make it **obedient** to Christ.*
>
> —2 CORINTHIANS 10:5, Emphasis Added

Because of our old nature and the devil's lies, it is easier to remember the bad stuff that happens in our lives. For example, when you take a long-planned trip where you have labored over every detail and when you return, the most dominant memories tend to be of the misfortunes or of the disappointments that we suffer on this trip.

Why is negativity such a struggle and our automatic default when it's God's will for us to maintain a positive outlook and to be thankful in all things? According to Coach Tomlin of the Pittsburgh Steelers, "You remember the losses *more* than you remember the successes!"

As neurologist and therapist Rick Hansen explains in his best-seller, "We need to be aware of the negative bias—the human brain tends to be drawn to negatives, it has radar that notices danger before it can see something enjoyable. And because of our negative bias, we tend to remember all of the unfortunate experiences before we recount any positive experiences. Since neurons that fire together wire together, staying with a negative experience past the point that's useful is like running laps in hell: You dig the track a little deeper in your brain each time you go around it." Hanson warns that if we don't attend to and install positive experiences, "the brain's net will automatically keep 'catching negative experiences.'"[38]

GOOD NEWS

But there is good news—we can learn to think differently! And when we learn something new, we can *change* the neuron connectors in our brain! Every time we reactivate a circuit, synaptic energy increases and those links become more robust and easier to reactivate. Whenever we think new thoughts over and over again, they become stronger and more engrained. And then, over time—with repetition—they take up less brainpower.

We can actually harness, or take captive, the brain's plasticity by *re-training* our brain to make God-inspired positive pathways more automatic (repetition). When we choose to go that same pathway hundreds of times (repetition), slowly a road forms and it becomes defined and easier to navigate. When we deliberately think about our thinking, we have the potential to make a new pathway in our brain.

The Apostle Paul knew this by experience. And now science has proven it!

WHEN WE DELIBERATELY THINK ABOUT OUR THINKING, WE HAVE THE POTENTIAL TO MAKE A NEW PATHWAY IN OUR BRAIN. THE APOSTLE PAUL KNEW THIS BY EXPERIENCE. AND NOW SCIENCE HAS PROVEN IT!

We must train our soul's thoughts to respond to God's voice and become obedient to Him. We must capture the free-floating automatic thoughts that have dominated our old "mindset". We must make every thought line up with what God says. We must choose new God-inspired and hopeful thoughts and dwell on them. We must say them in our mind, and if necessary, even say them out loud. The brain is so powerful that it has the potential to make changes on its own, but this process becomes even more intensified when we ask the Holy Spirit to add His power. We provide the desire and determination, and then the Holy Spirit makes it possible.

> *Those who live according to the flesh (soul/body) have their minds set on what that the flesh (soul/body) desires; but those who live in accordance with the **Spirit** have their minds (soul) set on what the **Spirit** desires. The mind (soul) of sinful man is death, but the **mind (soul) controlled by the Spirit** is **life** and **peace**; the sinful mind (soul) is hostile to God. It does not submit to God's law, nor can it do so. Those **controlled** by the sinful nature (soul/body) cannot please God.*
> —ROMANS 8:5-8, Brackets and Emphasis Added

The mind (soul) controlled by the Holy Spirit is life—not *death or destruction*, it is peace—not *chaos or worry*!

PULLING DOWN "STRONGHOLDS"

We must take down our own "Stronghold" for our self, leaving nothing standing—not even a stone. *I choose to take down my personal opinion (my will) and my preferences (destructive behaviors). I choose to take down lies (Satan) and my own faulty thinking (my old nature). I choose to submit to God's voice. I must choose to have a new "mindset!" A new "mindset" is always my choice!*

Here is the formula for pulling down our own stronghold:

DISTRESS: Recognize our pain from living in a fallen world!
DECIDE: Not to just live with it!
DESIRE: Be desperate for God's love and His perfect will!
DELIVERANCE: With God's help, *pull down* the "Stronghold!"
DILIGENCE: Take captive *every* thought!

I pulled down my own "Stronghold," and sometime later, the Lord gave my husband a promise. God told Phil not to feel guilty about me not being able to bear any natural children because God would fulfill me in many other ways. That's the way God works! He doesn't allow something to be taken from our lives that He can't make up to us in other ways. It is His grace!

> *God will repay you for the years that the locusts have eaten... You will have plenty to eat, until you are full, and you will praise the Name of the Lord your God, Who has worked wonders for you.*
>
> —JOEL 3:25-26

I have teased my husband through the years that I don't have *time* to be *more* fulfilled! I have been able to do more than I could ever have imagined, and I have been truly blessed! One of the most unexpected and exhilarating areas of my life is having the opportunity to spiritually "birth" women. A woman shared a connection that I had never made before. Her observation was, "You may not have given natural birth, but you have certainly given spiritual birth to many women!"

God truly does give us the desires of our heart. He will bring "good" out of every situation and will repay until "you are full"! How can I not trust my God with every detail of my life, when He has proven to be so faithful to me! I have learned to trust Him with my whole being—knowing how much He loves me!

It was decades later when my husband surprised me by asking, "Can you ever forgive me for you not being able to have children?" I was astonished, and I enquired why he would even ask that. I continued, "Did you forget God's promise to you about me?" He answered, "No, I thought you forgot it." Something in our conversation had triggered the "old mindset". His "old mindset" of wanting to be perfect was reacting to my "old mindset" of wanting everything perfect. It is so easy to go right back to that well-worn familiar pathway of automatic thoughts that formed our "Stronghold".

IT IS SO EASY TO GO RIGHT BACK TO THAT WELL-WORN FAMILIAR PATHWAY OF AUTOMATIC THOUGHTS THAT FORMED OUR "STRONGHOLD."

Now I am free to have a new "mindset"—but I must be diligent! We must be on guard because stress, trauma, and old wounds being opened again, can make us go right back to the more ingrained and worn original pathway, toward our "Stronghold." Back to being "frozen in time!" Back to our familiar automatic thoughts—back to our old "mindset". This "Stronghold" had become rubble on the ground but could quickly be re-built into that "Stronghold" once again!

GET UP OUT OF YOUR CHAIR!

I knew that Phil was just about ready for his *"Happy Dance!"* Phil had been searching his heart and life, and God revealed to him that his struggle was trying to "understand" God. He was working through this process with God when we had an unexpected visit from our son. He was living about twelve hours away, so we could not spend as much time together.

When I learned that Brent was coming for a visit, I had an idea. Because Brent has had many struggles, I knew that the devil would be plaguing him with guilt and shame. I wanted him to have in his mind a visible picture of our unconditional love. I told Phil that I wanted us to physically "dance" around Brent to demonstrate our unconditional love and joy that he is our son. So whenever the devil would torment him and tell him of our disappointment or disapproval, Brent could shake his fist at the devil and say, "No sir! That's *not* true. My parents danced around me with their unconditional love." Phil just looked at me, and I knew by his silence that I had a reluctant dance partner.

Phil took off work and for five days our son poured out his heart to us. It was an amazing and God-ordained time. In his sharing, we got a glimpse into the real Brent. He revealed to us his frustrations and his fears, but most importantly we got a glimpse of his heart—a genuine heart for God and others.

Brent would be the first to acknowledge that he is not always *Victorious* in spirit, soul, and body. And because of this, he is humbled to be used by God and to speak to those in need wherever he goes. Phil and I were moved to tears by Brent's heart. Later, I said to Phil, "Isn't Brent's heart amazing? You and God did that! God knew what He was doing when He decided you should be Brent's dad. Brent needed your God-influence so he could see Jesus!" And on that day, Phil didn't feel like a failure as Brent's dad. It was confirmation that he had been a good dad after all—in the area that mattered most!

The next day was to be Brent's departure. That morning we were in deep conversation, and I shared with Brent my idea and that I wanted us to "dance" around him. He looked over at his dad, and there was Phil with a look of dread. Brent jumped up and said, "Okay, Dad, get up out of your chair. I don't want to do this, and I can see that you don't either, but let's do it for Mom!" My reluctant dance partner got up, and we danced around Brent, telling him of our love. During our dance, Brent said, "Pick up your feet, Dad!" Phil did, and we had a joyful and blessed time of celebration with tears streaming down all our faces.

We took Brent to the train station, and on our way home we stopped at one of my favorite places, See's Candies. It was just a few days before Easter and the place was packed. The See's lady was so gracious and kind to two developmentally disabled young men ahead of us—who had just come in to get a sample! We were next in line, and we told her how impressed we were with her kindness.

As she took our order and filled our box, we engaged in conversation. She then asked us how long we had been married. We told her, and she looked at me and said, "What's your secret?" I said, "I finally stopped expecting my husband to change, and instead, I wanted to change!" She asked, "Are you Christians?" When we told her that we were, she relayed that she was a P.K.—a preacher's kid! I said, "Me too!" She said, "But I couldn't wear make-up or even pants!" I said, "Me too!" She confided that she was just finding her way back to the Lord.

She wanted to know how we would like our candy box wrapped, and we replied, "We don't need it wrapped at all." And then she did a "Happy Dance" right there in the middle of See's Candies. She had such rhythm and swagger, and I whispered to Phil, "*That's* how you do a *"Happy Dance!"* We both giggled, knowing what I was "hinting". She handed us our candy, and Phil told the See's lady what I said. She looked at us for a moment and then replied, "You guys are the Christians—you should be teaching me how!" And then she did another "Happy Dance!"—right in the middle of chaos and congestion!

As we went to our car, we looked at each other and said, "What just happened? Did she say we should be teaching her how?" We both knew that God had spoken to us through the See's lady! God was saying, "Get up—and do *'THE Happy Dance!'* And then go and teach others how!"

Phil's soul and mind finally agreed with his Holy Spirit-infused spirit. Finally, he didn't have to "understand". He just had to agree with God—and instruct and have his own soul affirm that God really does know best! And that day, Phil was finally ready to add the final dimension—he was ready to even "rejoice" and celebrate God's plan! Phil pulled down more remnants of his "Stronghold!" The reluctant partner became eager to participate in *"THE Happy Dance!"* And he did!

"THE Happy Dance" can't occur with a reluctant partner. It requires the synergy of our spirit, soul, and body! *"THE Happy Dance"* requires spirit, soul, and body to come into agreement. Like Brent conveyed to his dad, sometimes we have to say, "I know you don't want to, but get up out of that chair!" and "Pick up your heels!" Sometimes we have to tell our soul or our body, our reluctant partner, that it is time to get up and dance.

> *"THE HAPPY DANCE"* CAN'T OCCUR WITH A RELUCTANT PARTNER.

Someone asked us, "What does *"THE Happy Dance"* look like? Does it look like the Hokey Pokey or the Twist or something else?" The answer is "Something Else!" I can tell you that your dance probably won't look the same as the See's lady's dance! It is not about the moves, the rhythm, or anything technical! It is just a deliberate demonstration, a tangible expression of freedom and joy responding to "The Lord of the Dance!" It is a *private* moment of surrender and recognition and a response to being in the awesome presence of God. If we are "self"-conscious or worried about how it looks, it has just become about us—and not Him! I skip, some jump up and down, others employ graceful motions—it is *not* about *how* it is demonstrated.

The purpose of *"THE Happy Dance"* is desiring to worship God, "The Lord of the Dance", with the synergy of our spirit, soul, and body rejoicing in God's great unconditional love and awesome plan—past, present, and future! Rejoice in your freedom because the heavy load is gone—and the result is pure joy!

I am being TRANSFORMED... *By Pulling Down My Stronghold!*

Study Questions

1. The devil's strategy is to influence our thinking. He begins by pointing to and emphasizing a hurt, a lack, a need, or a desire. He tries to instill hopelessness so that we will listen to his false arguments and become driven by our old "mindset". Identify how the devil has tried this tactic on you and explain the outcome.

   Explain: _____

   _____

   _____

2. The definition for a spiritual "STRONGHOLD" is described on Page 84. Can you identify your own "STRONGHOLD(S)"?

   ☐ Shame   ☐ Need For Perfection

   ☐ Helplessness   ☐ Lack Of Acceptance

   ☐ Envy   ☐ Can't Measure Up

   ☐ Hopelessness   ☐ People Pleasing

   ☐ Unforgiveness   ☐ Feeling Insignificant

   ☐ Rejection   ☐ Repression of Deep Hurt

   ☐ Need For Approval   ☐ Never Satisfied

   ☐ Feeling De-Valued

3. The "STRONGHOLD" affects our emotions. Which detrimental feeling(s) have you experienced?

    ☐ Fear   ☐ Anger

    ☐ Resentment   ☐ Jealousy

    ☐ Pride   ☐ Sadness

    ☐ Self-Pity   ☐ Other "Self" Words

4. The product of these negative emotions take form in outward behavior. These are described on Page 85. Do you succumb to any of them?

    Explain: _____

    _____

    _____

    _____

    _____

    _____

5. How do my personal opinions and preferences impact my "STRONGHOLD"?

    _____

    _____

    _____

    _____

    _____

6. How does the devil's lies and my own faulty thinking impact my "STRONGHOLD"?

_____
_____
_____
_____
_____

7. How is a "STRONGHOLD" pulled down?

_____
_____
_____
_____
_____

8. What is your plan of action to not let your "STRONGHOLD" be built right back up when you experience stress, trauma, or an old wound being opened?

_____
_____
_____
_____
_____

THE Happy Dance

9. Read Psalm 144:1-2 and Psalm 37:39-40. Who is our real "STRONGHOLD"? How is He described in these verses?

_____

_____

_____

_____

_____

Chapter Six

Adulterous Emotions!

What if the ancient Biblical prophets of old were right when they proclaimed, our heart is *deceitful*—our heart plays tricks on us; and our heart is *difficult to really know*.[39] They were saying that our heart is *adulterous*—it is twisted and contaminated. Before we can become *Victorious*, we desperately need to be healed—spirit, soul, and body!

ADULTEROUS EMOTIONS

A word that describes a painful event in the lives of many is "Adultery". This word can have different meanings for each of us. To some, it represents an angry God shouting out a commandment. To others, it is a word that contains a warning of impending danger and consequences. For others, it is a word to ignore because there are no absolutes—so just do what makes you feel good or meets your need. To those who this poisonous snake has bitten—adultery conjures up a feeling of great pain, betrayal, anger, and unfathomable hurt. These people understand why the admonition "not to commit adultery" has been given—so that many could be spared from this excruciating experience.

This verse is also descriptive:

A man that commits adultery lacks judgment; whoever does so, destroys himself.

—PROVERBS 6:32

The word adulterous comes from the root of "adulterate", which referred originally to the defiling of the marriage relationship. But this word is also used to describe the process of debasing other aspects of life.

I *(Phil)* use the word "adulterous" to describe some of our emotions—because our emotions can be debased, diluted, spoiled, or become impure through the process of life, and the painful moments and events we have experienced—or have even just imagined.

I've heard it said that many individuals, particularly men, are unemotional—but that is not true. Every person on the planet has an emotional life. It is what we do with our emotions that are the primary and determining factor in our behaviors and our happiness. Some let their emotions flow freely, maybe too freely; others are uncomfortable with their own feelings, so they push them down.

I have worked as a prison psychologist for several years, and before I meet with an inmate, I review their paperwork. Usually, the information and diagnosis identify the patient with an anti-social personality disorder such as Paranoid; Schizoid; Antisocial; Borderline; Histrionic; Narcissistic; Avoidant; Obsessive-Compulsive; or Dependent.[40]

Adulterous Emotions!

In all of these personality types, there has been a severe adulteration of emotions. It may have been early childhood abuse, trauma, violence, prenatal alcohol or drug toxins, or a myriad of other difficulties that plague human beings. Just the mention of these disorders is a harsh reminder of the pain that many go through. All too often, they perpetuate this pain, as they then inflict it on others. It is due to adulterous infiltration that has diseased their emotional life.

Our emotional history may not be as tainted or severe as these people. But in our ongoing drama of life—what psychotherapist's call, our "play of consciousness"—our on-going movie can be a very painful one. Your degree of broken-heartedness or bruised ego may not reach the medical books. Still, to you, it has destroyed your joy and prevented you from having the happiness you can only dream about—and the thriving relationships you long to enjoy.

FEAR

When we ponder on the origins and etiology of human suffering, we move towards those root problems plaguing the human race. In all of life's stories, there is one common denominator: fear, or one of the derivatives of fear. I can still picture the feelings etched on the faces of the individuals I have counseled, both inside and outside of prison. Even if they appeared to be strong, often there was an underlying and pervading sense of fear that gripped them. Fear is tormenting and can create or lead us into physical and emotional pain.

FEAR IS TORMENTING AND CAN CREATE OR LEAD US INTO PHYSICAL AND EMOTIONAL PAIN.

Jesus warned that circumstances can, and will, arise in this world that result in "Men's hearts failing them from fear." (Luke 21:26)

Mark Twain once said, "I have been through some terrible times in my life, some of which actually happened." I am sure you would agree with Mr. Twain concerning the afflictions of worry, anxious thoughts, and phantom fears. Did you ever have phantom fears growing up as a child? They were the fears that were only imaginary or fictional in nature. When I *(Phil)* was nine years of age, I took over my big brother's paper route in the Los Angeles area. It was a distance from my house and required delivering papers every day and collecting the monthly bill from each customer. So due to the early Sunday morning route and collecting money during or after the route, I would often be out in the dark. Looking back now, it seems like a big responsibility for a nine-year-old, but for me, it was a normal way of life.

When I would leave the house for school, paper route, or other activities, my mother would *always* say, "Be careful!" That would be a customary admonition from a mother. But later, I realized that my mother always carried an above-average load of anxiety and fear because my mother lost a younger sister in a tragic car accident at a young age. And I believe her worrisome anxiety began to enter my mind. It was not my mother's intention, she had developed this "mindset" through her own experience, and I would soon follow suit. Eventually, I had to deal with the subtle and buried fear.

When I was collecting money or delivering newspapers in the evening, some strange things began to happen. I would see a tree or a bush in the distance, and my imagination would begin to perceive a different object. The tree would turn into a person, and that person would start to create a phantom fear in me. The more I focused on that fear, the more real that person became! I would eventually discover it was not an actual person, or if I wasn't sure, I would take off on my bike so quickly that he could never catch me.

My perception produced that "fight or flight" response—if the bush appeared to be a large dangerous man, I responded, and I was out of there! Now I might mention that although I was never robbed on my paper route, I later was robbed at other jobs at least eight times. In other words, the neighborhood in which I lived was not known to be a safe area. Even as a young child, two large young men came up to me while I was out Trick-or-Treating and roughed me up a little, and stole my bag of candy. So, there are times when phantom fears can be reality-based.

I enjoy walking and many times due to limited daylight hours, I often take short walks in the evening. And sure enough, when I am walking, I will look ahead and see a figure that may appear to be a human being. The difference between now and when I was a child is—now I am able to verify that the figure is only a tree. I don't become anxious or fearful, but instead, I can quickly extinguish any phantom fears and realistically evaluate my perceptions and change them. You may have heard the instruction, "face your fears," and this is a valid principle of life. Facing our fears gives us the opportunity to determine whether our fears are false or realistic. And this gives us insight on how best to handle them.

A few years ago, my wife and I led a teaching tour throughout the Middle East, Italy, and Greece. One day while touring Israel, we were at Masada, an ancient fortress, where the Israelites were fighting for their independence from the Roman Empire at a time in history. You take a tram car up the very steep mountain, but you must walk for the descent. As you look from the top of Masada, there is a valley way down below. You have to take a very narrow staircase trail to descend from the mountain

As Debby and I approached this trail to return to our bus, we saw that one of the women traveling in our group was shaking and crying. When we asked her what was wrong, she said, "I am terrified of heights and I came up here with you to overcome this fear." This woman had a phobia of heights, commonly known as Acrophobia. I once had this phobia and had overcome it, but my first thought was, "Why did you have to face it now—and here?" I happened not to be feeling very well that day and was barely surviving, and now we had to focus on somehow getting her down the mountain.

We put the woman in between us and had her place her hands on my shoulders, and then Debby held onto hers. To the chagrin of the tourists following behind, and with a lot of prayer and desperation, we walked this woman very slowly through the process of facing her life-long fear—one step at a time.

Fear is a concentrated, short-term bolt of anxiety. The amygdala is the portion identified in the brain that controls fear and anxiety. It is located deep within the brain, not far from the hippocampus, the area of the brain that controls memories and helps the brain learn and re-learn information. Although the fear response registers in the brain, we now know that fear affects not just the brain but our entire being.

FACING OUR FEAR

We had been married only a week and had just returned from a wonderful honeymoon in San Francisco. My new husband's car had broken down just before our wedding, so we had borrowed a car from my parents. After our car was repaired, I drove the 70 miles back to my parent's home to pick up our car and take back the rest of our wedding gifts. The wedding gifts wouldn't all fit in my car, so my

Adulterous Emotions!

brother offered to fill his car with the extra gifts and follow me back to my new home.

As we began the drive to my new home, it started raining "cats and dogs." Before I knew what was happening, my vehicle hit standing water on the freeway and began to hydroplane. My car began to spin, and when it finally came to rest, it had taken out 30 feet of fence and sat only a yard away from a power pole. God had His hand on me that day, and I walked away without a scratch, and not even one wedding gift was damaged!

I felt terrible having just ruined my new husband's repaired VW Bug. The picture of my wrecked car even made the newspaper—it must have been a very slow news day in Bakersfield, California. Under the picture was the caption, "Deborah Zoe Sloan, 19—married a week to Rev. Phillip Sloan—got an unwanted bridal gift last night when her car skidded near McFarland and ripped out 30 feet of fence. She was unhurt." I was scared to death, embarrassed, and humiliated. It was definitely a traumatic event!

One of the outcomes of the accident was that I became terrified to ever drive in the rain. Fortunately, we were living in Southern California, so I was able to avoid it most of the time. About six years after the accident, my mother visited us, and we drove to Los Angeles for a shopping day. On the way home, it started to pour. It was dark, and the road looked so slippery to me. I began to pull over so that my mother could drive the rest of the way home. My mother used her firm "mother voice" and said, "No, you are not going to pull over! You are going to drive—if you don't do it now, you never will get over this!" I was experiencing a panic attack, but she prayed and talked me through a very difficult night.

She was really giving me the best Godly counsel! She was saying "do not give way" to your fear.[41] That night, I learned, with God's help,

I could drive in the rain—even when it was dark. It was good that God delivered me from that fear because later in our ministry, we lived in Portland, Oregon, where it seems to rain almost every day!

That day I became *Victorious* over my fear and took another step on my journey to *"THE Happy Dance!"* Who knows what would have happened had I remained stuck in that fear! Would it have settled in my heart and brain, causing a pattern for panic attacks? Would I have become trapped in that fear, keeping me in bondage for the rest of my life? Would it have become a root for fear to torment and grow? The fear response may begin in the brain, but as fear finds a home, it then inhabits the heart and the soul of a human being, as well as the physical body.

THE FEAR RESPONSE MAY BEGIN IN THE BRAIN, BUT AS FEAR FINDS A HOME, IT THEN INHABITS THE HEART AND THE SOUL OF A HUMAN BEING, AS WELL AS THE PHYSICAL BODY.

I did not have to remain "frozen in time". I was able to move on and not have that fear control me. Not only did I have to deal with my emotions that night, but I had to respond with a physical act of driving to complete my deliverance. My spirit, soul, and body had to align to facilitate my newfound freedom.

UNFOUNDED FEAR

Our fear can also be ignited or exaggerated by our active imagination. How we perceive a situation can often lead to an anxious response—like seeing a "man" hiding, instead of a tree. There can be relatively small perceptions that lead to an imagination gone wild. When my wife was 20 years old, she was learning to play the organ for congregational singing in a church we were leading in Southern California. She was young and anxious in her new role as a pastor's wife, and that morning was diligently applying herself to reading the music—while adding bass notes and volume with her feet! At the end of the service, when she walked out to talk with some of the people in the congregation, she was confronted with a very harsh tone from a church member as she said, "You didn't even smile at me when you were up there playing the organ!"

OUR FEAR CAN ALSO BE IGNITED OR EXAGGERATED BY OUR ACTIVE IMAGINATION.

This woman, who was a board member's wife, felt Debby had ignored her. And my young wife was so focused on her new experience at the organ she was unable to acknowledge *anyone*! This woman had a fear of being rejected, and that day it was a phantom fear and became a false perception that was projected on Debby.

This woman was reacting from her "Stronghold" of not being accepted. It was fueled by fear. All the fears of living trace backward in time to an original source. The fear of death is the original starting place of tormenting fear. Fear then spreads its disgusting roots out into every intricate passageway and blind alleys of our being. This verse in the Bible vividly describes fear:

Since the children have flesh and blood, He (Jesus) too shared in their humanity so that by His death He might break the

> *power of him who holds the power of death—that is, the devil— and free those who all their lives were held in slavery by their fear of death.*
>
> —HEBREWS 2:14- 15, Brackets Added

The devil weaves his tentacles of fear into the foundation of *every* "Stronghold": Shame, Rejection, Anxiety, Fear, Need for Approval, People-Pleasing, Repression of Deep Hurt, Need for Perfection, Envy, Can't Measure-Up, Lack of Acceptance, Hopelessness, Helplessness, Never Satisfied, Feeling De-Valued, Feeling Insignificant, Unforgiveness, Bitterness, Self-Pity, Self-Hatred, and Rebellion.

Substance abuse, over-indulgence, and many other severe maladies often have their systemic roots in fear (i.e., fear of failure, fear of not measuring up, fear of being unloved and/or accepted, fear of remembering our past).

Jesus came to break the power of our "Strongholds" and free us from being enslaved by the devil and fear. As we allow God's love to permeate our being, He breaks the bondage and torment of our fear.

> *Love (God's love) has in it no element of fear; but perfect love (God's love) drives away fear, because fear involves pain...*
>
> —1 JOHN 4:18, Weymouth Translation, Brackets Added

ANGER

Anger is often defined as an emotion that is aroused within us for the purpose of preservation and protection. It can move way beyond the "fight or flight" from the "stalking cheetah" and our own survival, to become a divine detector of when our personal worth and dignity is threatened. Anger becomes that fire in our soul that rises up when we are intimidated by our surroundings and say, "I am made to be valued, not de-valued. God made me to have dignity and honor!"

Anger is the tool to embolden ourselves to intentionally protect our personal worth, meet our essential needs, and maintain our basic convictions. This is the anger that is described in the Bible—*yes, be angry but do not sin!*[42]

But don't ever allow your anger to define you or limit your destiny! Rage is one of the uncontrollable siblings of anger and is often activated by trauma and is a seething boiling pot of buried anger.

> *Get rid of all bitterness, rage and anger, brawling and slander, along with every form of malice.*
>
> —EPHESIANS 4:31

While working on my doctorate, I *(Phil)* was directing a transitional housing program for teenagers who were wards of the court. Our responsibility was to provide them with independent living quarters in an apartment complex, assist them in completing high school, and help them to acquire personal skills to function in society. It was towards the evening hour when I received a call to pick up a seventeen-year-old from a juvenile facility in the mountains of Northern California. I arrived as they were distributing a small amount of clothing to a young, slender, ruddy-faced teenager. We were just getting acquainted as we began the way to his new home along a curvy mountain ride.

I was unaware at the time of the extent of this young man's rage and the cavernous furrows of pain that were dwelling within him. As we began to drive down from the mountain and view the green valley below, this young man broke the silence as we were winding around a treacherous curve. He broke the silence with these words, "This is the curve where my mother drove off and killed herself. They told me she was driving drunk and lost control of the wheel."

I could immediately feel the lingering pain and see the cold stare of abandonment that pervaded this young life. A life that should have been so filled with adventure but became stunted by a tragedy beyond his comprehension. He was a raging inferno inside, but you could feel the frigid chill of his hardened heart. He had become "frozen in time!"

Anger can start from minor irritability but can metamorphose into a murderous rage. Anger can heat up slowly and simmer, but eventually, it will manifest in outward problems or inner physical and emotional pain. Anger can become an adulterous and toxic emotion as it is contaminated by a seething hatred, as the first family experienced with Cain towards his brother, Abel. Cain was driven by an inner turmoil that led to a murderous rage that resulted in a tragedy. Because of this, he became a marked man, due to the adulterous emotion of anger escalating into rage. How different the story could have been if this powerful emotion could have been turned around with forgiveness and cooperation. Freedom and gratitude could have flowed instead of the blood of an innocent brother.

ANGER CAN START FROM MINOR IRRITABILITY BUT CAN METAMORPHOSE INTO A MURDEROUS RAGE!

Adulterous Emotions!

Sometimes our adulterous emotions are *not* the product of trauma, great injustice, or deep emotional wounds. Often our emotions have become a snare because we have learned to react or behave in habitual or destructive patterns. Pushing down our anger and letting it smolder is just as detrimental to our own physical and mental health as explosive anger is. Our pent-up anger leaves aftershocks that ripple through our whole life and world. Could it be that our rage might even manifest in physical symptoms with unexplained medical conditions?

OFTEN OUR EMOTIONS HAVE BECOME A SNARE BECAUSE WE HAVE LEARNED TO REACT OR BEHAVE IN HABITUAL OR DESTRUCTIVE PATTERNS.

What makes you angry? Your life's filter system is reacting, and this could be a warning signal that there is a "Stronghold" that needs to come down! Which "Stronghold" is residing behind that anger?

PSYCHOLOGY'S ANSWER

Various disciplines from Hippocrates, Plato, Freud, Frankl, Jung, Maslow, Rogers, and a myriad of others have attempted to understand the physical and psychological condition of a man and a woman—to find out what makes us tick.

They have explored disease, depression, anxiety, distress, abuse, hysteria, psychosis, and many other disorders that plague the human soul and body. They have discovered the aberrations of many of the delicate aspects of the human condition, and from their limited perspective, have developed procedures and plans to alleviate the suffering.

The latest brain research has developed a new phrenology to treat the brain. At the same time, Psychiatry has attempted to medicate the brain to alleviate the pain of depression, mood swings, psychosis, and other behavioral aspects of those who suffer from mental illness. Although many find some relief in these treatments, the human condition is still in need of another answer that all these professions cannot seem to find.

Although the roots of psychology and psychiatry trace back through the centuries, modern psychological treatments have only a brief span of research and history. The new evidence-based research finds that many of the current treatments are falling short of their intended results. Paradigm shifts occur in the realm of science and the study of objective and subjective human behavior.

With knowledge come paradigm shifts and new perceptions of human understanding and breakthroughs. Paradigm shifts, new thinking replaced by another, have occurred throughout the history of the study of human behavior.

Are we controlled only by our brains?

Can depression be cured by changing our chemical compositions?

Are we controlled by our mind or our instincts?

Are humans unique, or can the research results on mice always be translated to human behavior?

Are the mind and body interconnected or separated?

There is a need to continue to explore all avenues for health and healing. The field of psychiatry and psychology needs to be honest with itself. The trite saying of "If it ain't broke, don't fix it" needs to be, "It *is* broken and let's continue to explore how to fix it." The rates of depression, suicide, and abnormal behavior continue to escalate in our country and abroad, so answers are still needed as we endeavor to heal the broken-hearted and those contaminated with harmful emotions.

Dr. Robert Berezin, a psychiatrist, writes this: "The underlying theory of somatic psychiatry is that the source of human struggle is considered to be the *brain* itself, rather than the *person*. Treatments that follow from this simplistic, mechanistic and reductionist notion have been to act directly on the brain, always with violating and destructive outcomes. The real source of human suffering is not the *brain*. It is the *person*, the human being, in the context of damage to the play of consciousness."[43]

To summarize, our maladies, many times, are created by—things that happened to us, are done to us, or are perceived by us. True *transformation* occurs when we take the time to rectify the painful events, faulty perceptions, and lies of the enemy of our soul that continue to play whenever we attend the cinemas of our life—and the same movie is playing over and over again. Now is the time to not remain "frozen in time," but to allow the Holy Spirit to re-write the script!

POWER OF FORGIVENESS

Forgiveness has always been a difficult process for those who have been offended and damaged by the words or the actions of others. When we are in great pain or distress over a situation that has greatly affected our life, especially when it appears that someone has gotten away with their reckless words or inappropriate actions—we simmer in anguish and won't let it go. When thinking about how to respond, forgiveness is not usually our initial reaction (and to be quite honest, not our secondary either).

Many men grow up with false perceptions or interpretations of what their father should be like. He should love sports like Joey's father and should be there at all my games. He should gush over my grades like Billy's dad. He should ruffle my hair and tell me how much he loves me just like Danny's dad. As we have learned, our perceptions—though they can be false or imperfect—can easily become our reality throughout life. We can create an expectation of the father we desire that may not apply to our father. We may want our father to be "cool", "athletic", "good looking", "brilliant", or "strong". Many fathers would love to be all of those qualities but are unable to meet those expectations.

I *(Phil)* was a teenager, it was a Saturday evening, and my older brother and I were playing on a very competitive fast pitch softball team at Los Angeles Harbor College. This was a crucial game, and the team we were playing from another city was eager to win. My brother, David, was pitching, and I had the opportunity to catch for him. It is a position that I had played before and later would play in college. I was excited and motivated because my dad was sitting in the stands. I learned to play baseball with friends and coaches at the local park, and to my knowledge, my dad had never been at any of my games before.

My brother pitched a great game, and I was fortunate to have four hits that evening—I went 4 for 4 with an additional walk to round the bases. I was so excited each time because my dad had never seen me hit a ball before. That night we won the game and, with it, the league championship. After the game, my dad came up to me, as I was inwardly (and probably outwardly) beaming, and he said, "Didn't David pitch a great game!" My heart sank as I received no words of approval or recognition of my performance. And unknown to me at the time, another disappointment was added to a cauldron of bitter feelings boiling in my soul. My perception and expectations of my father were once again tarnished, and another brick was added to my wall of resentment. I was "frozen in time!"

Years later at the age of 33, while pastoring a church in Ventura County, I was thirsting for changes in my life. A mentor of mine came into my home and began to pray for me. He felt a strong sensing that I was carrying a burden too heavy to handle and asked me if I needed to forgive my father. My heart burst, and my spirit bore witness that there was deep and hidden pain within my soul.

I did not realize how the hurts had added up and left me "frozen in time!" Walls can take minutes to build but years to tear down! We need *transformation* that transcend human ability, ingenuity, and man-made solution.

WALLS CAN TAKE MINUTES TO BUILD... BUT YEARS TO TEAR DOWN!

Deep forgiveness requires that we finally let go of the painful memories and those responsible for those memories. Often, it is helpful to go back to the painful event in our mind, and by faith—forgive them, pray for them, and release them.

Forgiveness is not condoning the offense or the offender. Forgiveness is releasing the pain and hurt from your life—and trusting God to take over. If you find it difficult to even imagine how to do this, we suggest that you find a trusted confidant to help you walk through the process. Both Debby and I needed someone to walk us through the steps that bring cleansing and forgiveness.

I responded and forgave my father for all the years of bitterness and resentment that I had buried in my heart towards him. A release came, and I also experienced forgiveness and freedom in spirit, soul, and body.

Just a few days later, an event occurred that had never happened before. My dad called me on the telephone! He said that he had been thinking about me and asked me how I was doing!

This illustration is a demonstration of the power of forgiveness—something is broken and then released in the spirit realm. Since this phone call was the first time that my dad ever reached out to me, I was shocked and blessed, and a new beginning sprang forth in our relationship. To be honest, we never became best buddies or even had a strong relationship, but from that point forward I was free to love and understand him.

THIS IS A DEMONSTRATION OF THE POWER OF FORGIVENESS—SOMETHING IS BROKEN AND THEN RELEASED IN THE SPIRIT REALM.

A few years later, my dad gave me, my wife, and my son a special gift—he invited us to take a trip with him that spanned over 10 countries. It was an unbelievable gift and experience of a lifetime. It is a memory that is sealed in all our hearts forever. I was free due to the power of forgiveness that only God could provide. Forgiveness is the freedom that Christ brings through the cross. It changes our perceptions and expectations and provides a new direction on the highway of holiness. The soil of my heart was being prepared for my *"Happy Dance!"*

COULDA, SHOULDA, WOULDA

Sometimes it is easier to forgive others than to forgive ourselves! Most of us have feelings of regret, remorse, and regressing into old painful personal memories. Have you ever found yourself saying, I could have done… I should have done… or I wish I would have done…? This triad of regret that many hear will color your world with misery and potential depression.

We often find ourselves agreeing with "the accuser of the brethren," the devil himself. We can be drawn to our own negative bias and amplify our short-comings and failures with or without his voice.

There is an answer to this malicious self-slander. God has forgiven us of all of our past. May we encourage you to take an inventory of all your past failures and regrets, and feelings of not measuring up and let it go! Forgive yourself! And finally, be free from condemnation and from fear!

GO TO GEHENNA!

Right outside the ancient walls of Jerusalem is a valley. In Hebrew, it is called the valley of Hinnom, or in Greek, Gehenna. Gehenna is the word from which the concept of *hell* originated. After the Jews returned from Babylon, they turned this valley into the city dump, where they burned their garbage—or anything considered unclean. For that function, they kept a fire that was left continually burning. On my visits to the Holy Land, I have looked out upon this valley. From Gehenna, you can see the crucifixion site where the Savior of the World gave His life—and took care of all our toxic waste and garbage.

This valley is a constant reminder of the truth that God takes our junk and wasted lives and recycles them into a beautiful display of His righteousness. Jesus, our Lord, went to hell and back so we could be free of the toxins of sin and live a new life of right relationship with our Maker and with others. Our toxic waste comes in contact with His redemptive love, and that love *transforms* us into a new creation.

THIS VALLEY IS A CONSTANT REMINDER OF THE TRUTH THAT GOD TAKES OUR JUNK AND WASTED LIVES AND RECYCLES THEM INTO A BEAUTIFUL DISPLAY OF HIS RIGHTEOUSNESS.

As we take this journey of healing together, we must gather all the toxic waste and adulterous material that we needlessly carry. There is already Someone, our precious Lord and Savior, who has gone outside the city gates and prepared a place to dump your garbage and be free!

> *And so, Jesus also suffered outside the city gate to make the people holy through His own blood.*
>
> —HEBREWS 13:12

I encourage you to take all offenses, hurts and disappointments, and the contaminating influence of adulterous emotions, and put them on the Ash Heap and tell them to *"Go to Gehenna!"* As you respond to the spotlight of your spirit's Conscience, throw the unnecessary toxic waste on the Ash Heap and learn to control your adulterous emotions—you will begin to establish an atmosphere of peace, joy, and fulfillment.

In this healthy environment, you can be *Victorious*—in spirit, soul, and body! Because of the healing power of "The Lord of the Dance"—you can be free to experience *"THE Happy Dance!"*

> I am being TRANSFORMED... *By Burning My Trash...*
> *By Being Healed— Spirit, Soul, and Body!*

Study Questions

1. I use the word "adulterous" to describe some of our emotions—because our emotions can be debased, diluted, spoiled, or become impure through the process of life and the painful moments and events we experienced or have just imagined. Can you identify?

    Explain: _____

    _____

    _____

    _____

2. Some let their emotions flow freely, maybe too freely! Others are uncomfortable with their own feelings and push them down! Which are you more prone?

    ☐ Let your emotions freely flow.

    ☐ Push your emotions down.

3. What occupies your mind when you are awake in the middle of the night or during quiet times?

    Is it ☐ Faith OR ☐ Fear?

4. Do you have unhealthy fears?

   ☐ Yes OR ☐ No

   How does your fear manifest?

   ☐ Anxious thoughts   ☐ Panic attacks
   ☐ Life-long fear   ☐ Paranoia
   ☐ Fear of the future   ☐ Tendency to worry
   ☐ Fear of failure   ☐ Fear of rejection
   ☐ Other

5. Did you grow up in a fearful or anxious atmosphere?

   ☐ Yes OR ☐ No

6. What causes the greatest fear within you?

   Explain: _____

   _____
   _____
   _____
   _____
   _____
   _____
   _____

Adulterous Emotions!

7. What makes you angry?

- ☐ Certain People
- ☐ Your Circumstances
- ☐ Interruptions
- ☐ Frustrations
- ☐ Not Able to be in Control
- ☐ Delays
- ☐ Disappointments
- ☐ Lack of Resources
- ☐ Struggles in Marriage
- ☐ Conflicts at Work
- ☐ Other

8. When you are angry do you most times:

☐ Push it down and let it smolder   OR   ☐ Let it explode

9. Anger is your life's filter system that is reacting, and this could be a warning signal that there is a "Stronghold" that needs to come down! What "Stronghold" is residing behind that anger?

Explain: _____

_____

_____

_____

_____

10. Does forgiveness come easily for you?

☐ Yes   ☐ No

11. Do you have more of a tendency to:

☐ Hold grudges   OR   ☐ Easily let go of offenses

THE Happy Dance

12. Do you have someone right now that you need to forgive?

    ☐ Yes   ☐ No

13. Do you need to forgive yourself?

    ☐ Yes   ☐ No

14. Have you ever needed someone to forgive you?

    ☐ Yes   ☐ No

15. Have you experienced the emotional relief that comes when you have forgiven and shown mercy?

    ☐ Yes OR ☐ No

    Explain: _____

    _____
    _____
    _____

Chapter Seven

The Body Keeps Score!

Just the mention of the word "body"—the third part of our triune being—makes men and women everywhere tense up and then let out a collective, "Oh no!" We either obsess over it or try hard to push it from our consciousness. Just talking about our bodies can make us extremely uncomfortable.

GOD CARES ABOUT MY BODY?

The body is our physical house. It is the first expression of ourselves that anyone sees. Often judgments are made on that first impression. Is our body really that big of a deal, and is our Creator God even concerned about our body?

> *They (our bodies) were made for the Lord, and the Lord cares about our bodies."*
>
> —1 CORINTHIANS 6:13 NLT, Brackets Added

This scripture confirms that our Creator Father and our Designer Dad does care about the condition of our body.

God is concerned about how we treat our body—because it influences our whole life. Our bodies impact our health, our relationships, our families, our careers, our ministries, and even our worship of God. My body is my responsibility!

I *(Debby)* must admit that in the past, I did not understand this spiritual phenomenon. I knew I felt better about myself when I had a balanced diet and was exercising, but I didn't realize that our well-being had such a spiritual significance as well. As I have matured physically and spiritually, I now see a direct correlation between the two. How can I be everything God has designed me to be if I don't also attend to the physical realm of my being? Yes, we cry out for God's help and intervention when there is a need for His healing from illness and disease. Yes, we fall on our knees when we need to feel His strength to get through the day. Yes, we know that God has our best interest at heart and that He will heal our physical bodies.

But on the day-to-day, we tend to rely on our self and our own self-evaluation. It is up to us what we do or what we *don't* do to our own bodies. We do not see that aspect as being spiritual. We don't fall down before our God and ask for His guidance. We don't appeal to our God for a greater anointing of His influence and direction. We just go on our merry—or not so merry way! We don't realize how important our body is to our spiritual life because we do not understand our body's impact on our spirit, and especially our soul. We must get over our insecurities and apply the honesty that we discussed in Chapter Two. We need to take our bodies seriously.

Our body should not be exalted! *Nor* should our body be ignored!

OUR BODY SHOULD NOT BE EXALTED! *NOR* SHOULD OUR BODY BE IGNORED!

Past generations would not understand our take on the body. I don't think they would believe how much our culture emphasizes the body; whether it is indulging it (food and beverages, uppers and downers, clothes and attire, cosmetic procedures) or making the body excessively fit (diets, exercise, gyms, classes, marathons, steroids, and supplements) or abusing it (habits, addictions, anorexia and obesity, self-mutilations). Yes, even body sculpting! All these outward practices are ways to make us feel better about ourselves.

We have insecurities and long for perfection. Some try to obsessively improve the outer man; others give up and just want to ignore it. But both are indulgences of our flesh—because both are consumed with *"me"* and my own concerns! Whether we ignore our body, obsess and whip the body into shape, or indulge and give it anything that it desires—our body becomes a reflection of our spirit and soul.

And our soul is a reflection of our spirit and body. So, we can't leave one part of our being out of the equation. As we previously discussed, we can't be Victorious with a reluctant partner. And ultimately, because *each* area reflects our devotion to our God and becomes our testimony to the world!

WHAT ARE WE DOING TO OUR OWN BODY?

Our body expresses what is going on in our inner man (spirit/soul). Our body keeps score! Our soul's feelings and emotions impact our body. And if we don't deal with our toxic emotions, we put undue harm on our own bodies. Then to top it all off, you add unresolved issues, frustrations, worries, and concerns—what we call life!

This is called stress! I understand stress. There have been times when I *(Debby)* could not even fall on my knees to intercede because my pain and concern overwhelmed my faith! I knew what this stress was doing to my emotions and mental state, but I didn't know what the stress was doing to my body. I never even considered that!

Many studies have proven that the emotions we feel—can manifest in our physical well-being.

- In a ten-year study, individuals who could not manage their emotional stress had a 40 percent higher death rate than non-stressed individuals.[44]
- A Harvard Medical School study of 1,623 heart-attack survivors concluded that anger, brought on by emotional conflicts, doubled the risk of subsequent heart attacks compared to those who remained calm.[45]
- Fear triggers more than fourteen hundred known physical and chemical stress reactions and activates more than thirty different hormones and neurotransmitters."[46]

We have all experienced the "Fight or Flight" response— "I have to stay right here and defend myself" or "run like H____!" It is our body's interpretation of intense emotion—fear.

OUR BRAIN CANNOT DISTINGUISH BETWEEN REAL DANGER AND EVERYDAY STRESS.

Our brain cannot distinguish between real danger and everyday stress. When the brain senses stress, the response produces adrenaline and sends it out throughout the body and even to your organs and tissues. You sweat, your bronchial tubes open to permit more oxygen, and your heart rate will rise.

And we wonder what stress could be doing to our bodies! Stress causes you not to think clearly or respond with the right amount of intensity. Stress makes my hunger shut down, and stress causes Phil to reach for food.

Hormones are meant to be released in a balanced way. Just ask any woman, or any man married to a woman, how important this is!

"Adrenaline is a stress hormone that produces a 'high' as powerful as that of any drug (or narcotics). Elevated levels of adrenaline can make a person feel great. The person who has adrenaline pumping through his body has a lot of energy, needs less sleep, and tends to feel very excited about life in general. It focuses the brain, sharpens eyesight, contracts muscle in preparation for fight or flight."[47] Adrenaline can even be addictive!

Adrenaline is powerful, and when stress is *short-lived*, adrenaline is a positive addition to your life. The explosion of adrenaline is followed by fatigue, which then requires rest for the body and soul.

The problem is that the body cannot differentiate between real danger and stressful anger. It doesn't know if your life is in danger or that you are just yelling at your out-of-control teenager or the crazy driver. If the flow of adrenaline is excessive, such as when there is long-term stress, it can damage the body. An example of long-term stress could even be defined as living or working for years in an environment that makes you upset and angry. Being in this environment can form patterns in our behaviors—reinforcing how we react in given situations.

Excessive adrenaline causes mood issues, including anger, depression, irritability, lack of energy, trouble concentrating, sleeplessness, headaches, and mental problems, including anxiety disorders and panic attacks.

Elevated adrenaline levels are also known to cause increased blood pressure, increased heart rate, higher cholesterol, and risk of a heart attack. In the immune system, there is a reduced ability to fight and recover from illness. It can produce stomach cramps, reflux, and nausea. It can cause aches and pains in the joints and muscles. It also lowers bone density.[48] It causes an elevation in triglycerides (fats in the body), a height of blood sugar, blood to clot faster (contributing to plaque), the thyroid to become overly stimulated, and the body to produce more cholesterol. "All of these effects are potentially deadly over time."[49]

Whenever adrenaline is released, it is also accompanied by another hormone, cortisol. Over time, when high cortisol levels are released into our system, it also causes insulin and blood sugar levels to rise. Triglycerides and cholesterol levels in the bloodstream increase and remain elevated. Too much of the cortisol hormone is often responsible for weight gain and retention, particularly in the midsection.

Continually elevated cortisol levels have been shown to decrease serotonin, a chemical messenger that's believed to act as a mood stabilizer and help produce healthy sleeping patterns and boost your mood. Impaired immune function—and a faulty immune response have been linked to a wide range of diseases. Reduced glucose utilization—a significant factor in diabetes and weight control—increased bone loss—which has implications for osteoporosis. Reduced muscle mass and inhibits skin growth and regeneration, which are directly related to strength, weight control, and the general aging process. Increase in fat accumulation. Increase in blood pressure. Impair memory and learning and destroy brain cells.[50]

In short, "When long-term emotional stress continues and reaches the chronic level, the results of the continual production of these hormones become even more destructive. This is when toxic emotions become deadly emotions. The body begins to damage itself."[51]

Problem areas that are destructive to the body while living with stressful situations also apply to the "Adrenaline Junkie," who is always seeking pleasure. Adrenaline junkies may have one or more of these traits: they have to have one new experience after another, they are thrill-seeking and always looking for excitement, or they are involved in fast-paced and high-octane occupations. They have to maintain a continual high, and when they come down, they will even have severe withdrawals. The result is the same. Our bodies cannot handle these hormones perpetually flowing.

Long-term stress has been linked to anxiety disorders, panic attacks, post-traumatic stress disorder, depression, phobias, and obsessive-compulsive disorder.[52] It is also linked to physical diseases: heart and vascular problems, gastrointestinal problems, headaches (migraine and tension), skin conditions, pain and inflammation, lung and breathing issues, and immune impairment.[53]

NEGATIVE STRESS

Stress impacts our body, mind, emotions, and behavior. What are our emotions and lifestyle doing to our bodies?

Do you not know that your bodies are members of Christ Himself?

—1 CORINTHIANS 6:15

God has been holding me *(Debby)* accountable for my body and its health. The food I eat and its nutritional value, exercise, and rest—and now God has made me accountable for handling stress in my life. Now that I have discovered how detrimental stress is to my emotions and body, I realize that I must do something about it. Can I really control my life? Can I manage my own stress?

My regular dentist was out with a shoulder injury, and his replacement said that I needed dental work and a crown. I had just had a crown done the year before, and it was a relatively painless event, and I was pleased with the outcome. But not this time!

After having my tooth prepared for the crown, a temporary was placed, and he told me to watch what I ate and return in two weeks for the permanent to be placed. When I returned in two weeks, the dentist soon discovered that the new crown would not work and began the procedure all over again. But this time, my gum was still very sore, and I experienced a lot of extra pain. He made a temporary crown again and, this time, sent me home to wait for three weeks. But during this waiting period, I was in pain. I got my new crown, and immediately it didn't look right to me, but my gums were so swollen I really couldn't tell.

After three months, I got a second opinion, and this dentist said I should go back to the one who initially did the dental work and get it re-done. Now, who would want to confront a doctor and then endure the procedure for the *third* time? So, I kept putting it off—but there was always this nagging thought that I needed to take care of it. One month turned into two, and two turned into three.

God finally got through to my spirit, *"You are creating stress by not confronting the dentist—just get it over with, check it off your mind's list, and be free of it."* I could no longer ignore it—it was a mandate! This was one stress I could manage. It was a reminder; how many other stresses am I accumulating or creating by simply not managing them?

"Stress is the body and mind's response to any pressure that disrupts their normal balance. It occurs when our perceptions of events don't meet our expectations, *and we don't manage our reaction to the disappointment."*[54] Other than "fight or flight" situations, our stress is the result of, and can be summed up in two words—our *expectations* (soul) and our *reactions* (soul/body). Things don't meet our expectations, and then we don't manage our reaction to that disappointment. Sure enough, I am contributing to my own stress by not dealing with my expectations and my own reactions to them.

IT WAS A REMINDER; HOW MANY OTHER STRESSES AM I ACCUMULATING OR CREATING BY SIMPLY NOT MANAGING THEM?

"When Stress—that unmanaged reaction—expresses itself as resistance, tension, or frustration, throwing off our physiological and psychological equilibrium and it keeps us out of sync. If our equilibrium is disturbed for long, the stress becomes disabling. We fade from overload, feel emotionally shut down, and eventually get sick."[55]

Do you never have enough time in your day? Do you have unmet expectations? Do you have anger issues? Do you think that life or someone has treated you unfairly? Do you have tension or people in your life that are hard to handle? Could these bring strong emotion, add stress, and even impact your body?

THE VALLEY OF BACA

We could hardly wait to get settled in at our new church assignment. The church we were leaving was kind and gracious to us, and we had a lot of favor, but over half of our congregation was senior citizens, and we were barely thirty years old. The new congregation was predominately young and energetic and had a great hunger for God and spiritual renewal—and that was exactly where our heart was. As we met with the leadership at a home, they began asking difficult questions to my husband about where his leadership would take them. I was beaming from ear to ear because Phil was giving transparent and candid answers, and everyone seemed to be in perfect agreement. Let's get going to the Promised Land flowing with milk and honey!

With young fresh vision, the church began to grow. New converts from Mo-Town became part of the worship team, and there was excitement in the atmosphere, and the church was packed. Home Groups were introduced, utilizing mature and gifted leaders. We were so excited to see what God was doing and simply to be a part of it.

What happens when a young pastor has an old mindset of wanting to be perfect, and his young wife has an old mindset of wanting everything perfect meets difficulty in ministry? They travel

The Body Keeps Score!

through the Valley of Baca! You will inevitably experience pain and tears in ministry—simply because we are fallen creatures interacting with other fallen creatures.

We were experiencing a little heaven on earth. We loved our church; we loved our brand-new home and were so hopeful about what God was doing in our little world. And then the proverbial shoe dropped! Two board members asked for my husband's resignation because they didn't approve of all of the changes and our church's direction. They appealed to the denomination's leadership, and a meeting was scheduled.

The leader of the denomination had an abscessed tooth, had presided over another meeting that same evening, and was not on top of his game! After hearing from the two board members, he pulled my husband aside and simply advised him to resign as lead pastor, and he would do everything to find a new place for ministry. Fighting through the heartbreak and pain, my husband complied, and the following Sunday, the young pastor who so wanted to be perfect, resigned to the congregation. Talk about stress! And, of course, during this time of stress, the devil pulled out his weapon using the negative triad—fear, shame, and pain.

Most of the congregation did not have long-standing ties with the denomination, and they did not want to stay at that church with apprehensions that it could happen again. Fearing that they would be scattered, the nucleus asked us to stay in the area and start a new church. We were also very disappointed with the denomination since we believed we had a call to that community. My husband agreed to begin a new church, and with a mixture of sorrow and excitement, the Church of the Foothills was started.

Even though we had a large percentage of the congregation, God would not allow us to stay and take over the church property and

THE Happy Dance

facilities; it felt as if we would be hijacking the property from the denomination. Instead, God directed us to bless them and pray for them, and we found a Sunday home at the local Grange Hall. Even though we carried great pain in our hearts, we were delighted to be of one mind with all of our church. The unity brought peace to our troubled minds, and we began serving with excitement and anticipation. We were thriving in this environment, and going to church was inspirational *and* fun! Yes, rumors were flying around town about my husband, but they did not quench our knowing that we were exactly where God wanted us—in the community and the church we loved.

Three years later, I was looking out our front window and saw someone making their way to our front door—it was the deacon that had asked for my husband's resignation. He had been very unkind to Phil and had spoken despairingly to others about him. Why would he be coming to our home? Should I answer the door? If he had more unkind words to vent, I didn't want Phil to deal with him or get upset all over again. Phil was in his home office, and I did not want to alarm him, so I quickly answered the door. Ray asked if he could speak to Phil, but something was very different. The hostility was gone, and his eyes were soft; he even had an awkward smile. I quickly ran to Phil's office and told him of our unexpected guest. Phil said, "What could he possibly want? Let's go see!"

The words that Ray came to speak were unbelievable! He said, "I am here to apologize. I have watched you, and I was wrong about you. Our pastor just left our church, and we are in difficulty. I want you to come back and pastor our church!"

After all that had transpired, was I really hearing him correctly? As my husband accepted his apology, the two men embraced with tears streaming down their faces. My husband was moved and said he would consider and pray about his offer to return to the original church.

What Ray did not know is that God had just corrected my husband. As Phil was calling out to God and wanting to know what to do and how he could please God, God put his finger on something that had changed all of our lives. Phil sensed that God said, "You were in such a hurry to get to the Promised Land that you ran ahead with the young, the healthy, and the strong. But you left the feeble and the elderly behind. When I called My people to go to the Promised Land, they all went together—the young and the elderly, the feeble and the strong."

My husband knew exactly what the Lord meant, and he was convicted and was grieved in his spirit. Phil called out to God in repentance! And here, just a little while later, Ray is at our door! As Phil prayed, he knew what had to be done—but he would need God's special anointing to convince the leadership of our new church! They were delighted with our new church and loved the unity that existed there. Phil asked a difficult thing of them—to go backward and patiently bring everyone to the Promised Land together! It had been easier and more fun to run freely at our own pace and sprint to our desired destination! They didn't want to go back! But they had learned to respect and trust their young pastor. They were also willing to humble themselves to answer the Lord's prayer, *"Father make them one, as We are one."*

Within a few weeks, we were worshiping together. I heard Ray publicly apologize to my husband. I listened to my husband apologize. After all the lies and rumors swarming in our community and the denomination, my husband was publicly vindicated—I didn't really think that would happen until heaven!

The young pastor who wanted to be perfect and his young wife who wanted everything easy and perfect was growing up in the Lord—they were learning to trust God with every detail of their lives! In our Valley of Baca, our valley of tears, God was able to make it into a place of blessing! Only God can do that! God was even laying a foundation in our careers and finances. Phil was able to fulfill a dream of completing his Master's degree in Psychology. It was during this time that I was thrust into the field of design. And not only did we experience true reconciliation in the body of Christ, but Phil learned how to love and lead the *whole* body of Christ. Now, many years later, with the strong foundation that was laid, that church is "one" and is a healthy and vibrant church today.

Only God can take one of the most stressful times of our life, and our Valley of Baca became a valley of miracles!

> *What joy for those whose strength comes from the Lord, who have set their minds on a pilgrimage to Jerusalem. When they walk through the Valley of Weeping (Baca), it will become a place of refreshing springs. The autumn rains will clothe it with blessings. They will continue to grow stronger..."*
>
> —PSALM 85:5-7 NLT

HOW TO HANDLE NEGATIVE STRESS

Sometimes we, ourselves, are creating our own stress. If we don't deal with our emotions quickly, our brain cannot distinguish between a current event and a memory. If we continue to "nurse and rehearse" past hurts and grievances, we are adding stress because our body re-lives and "feels" the original pain all over again.

> **WHEN YOU ARE BETRAYED BY A MATE, FIRED BY A JEALOUS BOSS, ABUSED BY A CLOSE RELATIVE, OR MALICIOUS GOSSIP HAS DESTROYED YOUR REPUTATION OR CAREER—THE HEALING PROCESS CAN BECOME COMPLICATED. AND HOW LONG DOES IT THEN TAKE TO GET BACK TO NORMAL, IF YOU EVER DO?**

We also create stress when we don't respond to our own conscience or when we obsess over details or engage in "if only" and "it's just not right!" We put too much pressure on ourselves, and we magnify our own shortcomings. We often worry in advance! We make goals or deadlines that are impossible. Re-living a stressful situation is just that—it's stress! Consequently, our thought-life needs an overhaul. A change in attitude and focus is required.

But sometimes, the stress we are experiencing comes from other people or circumstances beyond our control. When you are betrayed by a mate, fired by a jealous boss, abused by a close relative, or malicious gossip has destroyed your reputation or career—the healing process can become complicated. And how long does it then take to get back to normal, if you ever do?

> **WE SOON DISCOVER THAT WE CAN NEVER CHANGE PEOPLE—AND OFTEN CAN'T CHANGE THE SITUATION THAT IS ADDING STRESS TO OUR LIFE.**

We soon discover that we can never change people—and often can't change the situation that is adding stress to our life. What is causing me to be stressed? Is it my expectations, or is it how I am reacting to them? So now, how do I spell stress? It is really *D-E-B-B-Y!* I am finally learning not to carry my stress with me continually, but to do my part, and most importantly—to give them to God!

> *Don't worry about anything; instead, pray about everything. Tell God what you need, and thank him for all he has done. Then you will experience God's peace, which exceeds anything we can understand. His peace will guard your hearts and minds as you live in Christ Jesus.*
> —PHILIPPIANS 4:6-7 NLT

During that most stressful period of our life, God revealed and proved that He would be "more than enough" to us. These three steps for handling stress became our new way of coping with life.

1. TURN YOUR STRESS INTO A "PRAYER AND PETITION" TO GOD!

The real answer to handling stress is inviting God into every situation! We must trust God with whatever is causing our stress—it is incorporating faith that God "is" and "will" work in this situation. Make faith declarations, even out loud, so that you are purposely reminding yourself not to be directed by your emotions—but instead to embrace the statements of your spirit's "Knowing" that God is in charge.

2. TAKE CARE OF YOURSELF—DO YOUR PART!

During times of stress, we need all the help we can get. We need more energy, strength, and vitality to be able to cope. We just looked at the negatives that stress inflicts upon our body; consequently, our body needs our special attention during times of stress. There are things that we can do to counteract the negatives upon our bodies.

- HEALTHY EATING — Eat regular meals instead of snacking or just getting by. Eat more vegetables, fruit, and fiber to enhance energy and digestive functions. Reduce salt, fats, and sugary foods, which have their own negative impact on our bodies.

- REGULAR SLEEP — Sleep is often compromised when stressed, but it is imperative for our mental well-being. Take time to relax and process your day *before* trying to sleep. It is advised to put your electronic devices away at least thirty minutes before trying to sleep. A warm bath thirty minutes before bedtime is beneficial; your body temperature rises when you are in the tub and falls when you come out. As the body temperature rises back to normal, sleep is induced. Reduce caffeine. A comfortable, cool, and dark environment help the body relax. If you have difficulty keeping stressful thoughts out of your mind, quote favorite scriptures and meditate on them instead of your concerns.

- EXERCISE — Exercise benefits your overall health and your sense of well-being. It also has some stress-reducing benefits. Physical activity helps increase the production of your brain's endorphins, your "feel-good" neurotransmitters.

Strenuous exercise requires your attention to be drawn to your body's movements and takes the focus away from your stress and the causes of your frustration. Walking can clear your mind. Take walks with God—converse and listen. Get out your earbuds and listen to God's Word or worship songs as you walk—it's good for your body and your soul!

3. PUSH YOURSELF IN THE RIGHT WAYS!

- ONE DAY AT A TIME...

So don't worry about tomorrow, for tomorrow will bring its own worries. Today's trouble is enough for today.
—MATTHEW 6:34

STRESS CAN MAKE YOU NOT THINK CLEARLY, OR FEEL OVERWHELMED, AND CAN EVEN IMPAIR YOUR THOUGHT PROCESS AND MEMORY.

Stress can make you not think clearly, or feel overwhelmed, and even impair your thought process and memory. Stress can also make it difficult to concentrate on tasks that need to be done—either making you overthink your problem or making you "shut down" so that you cannot think at all. So, the answer is, just concentrate on what you need to accomplish *today*. Don't worry about next week, next month, or next year. I have found that making a list for today helps me to clarify essential tasks from unnecessary ones. It keeps me focused and directed—and what a sense of accomplishment when I get to check it off! Since stress can also impair short-term memory, write more things down—that way, you don't have to worry about remembering and keep reminding yourself of details, events, or tasks.

- DON'T ISOLATE —

The words of the reckless pierce like swords, but the tongue of the wise brings healing.

—PROVERBS 12:18

When we feel overwhelmed, many tend to isolate and withdraw from people. But interacting with others can even assist in lifting the symptoms of stress. Find an encouraging and uplifting ear. Search out those who use discernment and share words of wisdom—you will walk away feeling refreshed and strengthened. Fresh eyes may even have new insight.

- REMEMBER TO SMILE —

A cheerful heart is good medicine, but a broken spirit saps a person's strength.

—PROVERBS 17:22, NLT

Smiling and laughing lifts your spirit and improves the way you feel. Remember to smile—and rejoice and celebrate God!

DREAD OR DELIGHT?

I am a certified trainer of officers and medical staff to help them recognize psychological symptoms within the prison population. As I walked into a packed classroom to begin my instruction, I suddenly was overtaken with stress and felt the beginning of a panic attack, but somehow, I made it through the lecture. After I completed the class, I walked back to my office and asked myself, what was happening to me? Why is something that I thoroughly enjoyed doing at one time, I now was dreading ever to do again?

As I was reading through Proverbs, my eyes became drawn to Proverbs 10:24. I realized the stress I was experiencing was coming from making poor choices. Instead of looking forward to the class, I began to dread what I once enjoyed. I discovered that there are two roads to travel. One road leads to stress; the other road leads to contentment. I found that this had been a pattern in my life for many years, and it was time to change!

Dread is a recipe for additional stress and anxiety. I chose to change this current pattern. I asked God to help me not dread future tasks but choose to delight in them. Dread or delight.

Dread can cause self-loathing, anxiety, and fatigue. Dread signals we are carrying the whole burden by ourself. Delight focuses our attention on the hope that God will intervene and give courage and wisdom. Choose to delight because God is with you! Will you dread tomorrow or look forward to the future?

What the wicked dread will overtake them; what the righteous desire will be granted.

—PROVERBS 10:24

Take delight in the Lord, and He will give you the desires of your heart.

—PROVERBS 37:4

DEALING WITH TRAUMA

In my practice at the medical office of the prison, I *(Phil)* frequently get referrals from doctors and nurses to treat patients that have reported somatic symptoms. These are symptoms that have no known organic origin. Many of my patients have somatic symptoms and panic attacks with no current diagnoses. Often they report feelings of having chest pain, extreme stomach pain, or severe back pain. Since I have experienced some bodily symptoms under extreme stress in the past, I have always been intrigued by the mind/body connection. After much research, I have developed treatment plans for these patients. I have learned from the experts in this field that dealing with emotional pain is essential, but there must be an avenue to free the body from past painful experiences.

We had a dear friend attending our church who had returned from Vietnam with a physical war injury. When Lee Craig returned from the war, he believed that his primary struggle would be dealing with the metal plate placed in his skull from a head injury. We learned together that the psychological scars and the emotional and physical trauma had caused him to be "frozen in time."

When this dynamic man came to our home for a Bible study, we had no idea what was going on inside of him. In the atmosphere of a loving group of people, this man unexpectedly moved from his usual demeanor to blurting out and expressing his great emotional pain. Lee was experiencing the negative triad of fear, shame, and pain, known as PTSD. We asked the Holy Spirit for wisdom on how to help him. We prayed for him, and the Lord revealed to our spirit that his painful memories had been "frozen in time," and he was unable to escape—because he didn't have an escape plan.

Part of Lee's healing process allowed God to deal with and heal the painful experiences in his spirit and soul. He received an immediate release, and that night deeply sensed God's healing grace. With a beaming smile, Lee said that he felt a peace that he hadn't experienced in years. Then he added, "But the test will be if I don't have to sit in the back row of our church!" His PTSD would manifest whenever he was in a crowd, so he felt comforted in the back row because no one could sneak up behind him.

Healing from trauma or other painful trials can only be completed when the body takes appropriate steps to finish the healing process. Because we are spirit, soul, and body—all three need to take part in complete healing. His healing came as he participated in three decisive steps.

- STEP 1 — With the prayer and support of his small group, he was able to take action and physically move to the third row of the church with a smile on his face. Lee also recounts, "I was meeting once a month with a group of 6-8 Vietnam vets at a pizza parlor. All of us squeezed into a corner booth so our backs could be to the wall. Cozy. I walked in the next Saturday, picked up a chair, and placed it on the outside of the table with my back to the room. That is where I sat from then on, and I was able to tell them why."
- STEP 2 — Lee requested to jump in the back seat of our car to go on an arduous sixteen-hour journey to attend a conference that had been extremely meaningful to other church members. There God revealed to him his purpose and ministry in life.

- STEP 3 — Lee went home and founded a local ministry to other vets that had also experienced painful scars from the war. He established a downtown location to be a healing center for these veterans. He also took a trip with other vets to Vietnam for healing and ministry.

We watched in wonder when this veteran moved from the back row of the church to the third row. And then, to the platform, to host a "Welcome Home" event at our church for all the Vietnam veterans in the area that had *never* been thanked for their service. It was a tearful and emotional event that will never be forgotten by any of us that attended. Lee was no longer "frozen in time" but was moving ahead—in his spirit, soul, and body! He had found his "missing piece!"

His story confirms the most recent research in trauma.[56] This research has discovered that healing from any type of painful experience—physical, emotional, or psychological—must also involve the physical body participating for the outcome to be complete. Since the body keeps score, the body needs to agree and become activated with a response—whether it be *"THE Happy Dance"* or moving to the third row of the church!

HEALING FROM ANY TYPE OF PAINFUL EXPERIENCE—PHYSICAL, EMOTIONAL, OR PSYCHOLOGICAL—MUST ALSO INVOLVE THE PHYSICAL BODY PARTICIPATING FOR THE OUTCOME TO BE COMPLETE.

I'm being *TRANSFORMED... By Taking Action to Be Free!*

Study Questions

1. Do you tend to obsess over your body?

    ☐ Yes ☐ No

2. Or do you rather try really hard to not think about your body or even push it from your mind?

    ☐ Yes ☐ No

3. The body is our physical house. It is the first expression of ourselves that anyone sees. What does your world see?

    Explain: _____

    _____
    _____
    _____
    _____
    _____
    _____
    _____

4. Do you think that life or someone has treated your unfairly?

    ☐ Yes   ☐ No

5. Do you have unmet expectations?

    ☐ Yes   ☐ No

6. Do you have tension or people in your life that are hard to handle?

    ☐ Yes   ☐ No

7. Do you have anger issues?

    ☐ Yes   ☐ No

8. Do you never have enough time in your day?

    ☐ Yes   ☐ No

Chapter Eight
It Tastes Sooo Good!

Paul stated to the Corinthian church that our bodies were made for the Lord! So, we should not be surprised that food became the first lure to draw us away from God—it is the same old movie—it was food that looked so enticing and appealing to Eve. She just had to have it!

Just like the original sin of the first woman, Eve, it is rebellion when we say, "I will decide, not God or anyone else, what goes into my own body. I will decide if it is bacon or kale. I will not be body-shamed into healthy living. My body is one area where I am totally in charge—I am the boss over my body!"

In the wilderness, the first temptation that the devil used to try and ensnare Jesus was food. It is so devious because the body needs the nutrients in food to exist. Food is not the culprit—we need food to sustain our life. Food should be a means to nourish our whole being—spirit, soul, and body.

THE Happy Dance

FOOD IS NOT THE CULPRIT—WE NEED FOOD TO SUSTAIN OUR LIFE.

But many Christians view food with a different purpose:

I get bored… so I eat!

I need something to soothe my emotions… so I eat!

I don't have much control—but I can control what I put into my body… so I eat!

I get stressed and don't know what to do… so I eat!

I need some fun… so I eat!

I don't want to feel my emotional pain… so I eat!

I'm in my car… so I eat!

I'm in my jammies… so I eat!

I'm watching T.V.… so I eat!

I'm in my bed… so I eat!

Food tastes sooo good… so I eat!

I need to celebrate… so I eat!

We are all "foodies" in my family… and so we eat!

"I have the right to do anything," you say—but not everything is beneficial. "I have the right to do anything"—but I will not be mastered by anything.

—1 CORINTHIANS 6:12-13

It Tastes Sooo Good!

A.W. Tozer said, "The abuse of a harmless thing is the essence of sin." For instance, food is necessary and harmless, but overeating and anorexia are both wrong because of the abuse that it inflicts upon our bodies. If our indulgences and overeating cause: self-consciousness, poor self-image, guilt, condemnation, poor health, or limits our energy or mobility—we are under the influence of our own soul and body. Or even the influence of the enemy of our soul, the devil.

It is not just an, "Oh well" or "It really doesn't matter." It does make a difference—in your physical health and well-being, in your productiveness to God's kingdom, and in your obedience to God.

I *(Debby)* grew up in an organized church with many rules and regulations. Women couldn't cut their hair, could only wear dresses, and couldn't wear make-up. Oh, by the way, where were the personal rules for the boys? None of us could drink alcohol or smoke, and we weren't allowed to swim or go to roller rinks together. The movie theater—yeah, that was a no! And of course, we could not dance!

My generation realized that all these rules did not have a biblical basis. There were so many rules and regulations. So, we threw them all out! But by throwing them all out, it seemed to give the church a free license to do anything! It was nobody else's business because we were finally in charge of our own life.

We had no rules! In the meantime, the Church became obese, Christians became alcoholics and substance abusers, Christians took up life-threatening habits, and the divorce statistics became the same as the un-churched. Sadly, we stopped talking about *real* biblical admonitions and wisdom.

My generation was so turned off by all the "no's" we didn't want any restriction, even those based on solid biblical restriction—restrictions that were given for our well-being and best interest. These biblical restrictions were not to deprive us but were given for instruction for our life to be blessed and enhanced.

The New Testament does not restrict us on what or what not to eat, how to dress, or our entertainment. But these are so much easier to check off a list and feel religious and even righteous! The Bible, however, is concerned with the heart (the real us), and our mind's thoughts, and our soul and body's responses and behavior. The Bible is concerned with our choices and our lifestyle because they impact our health and our relationship with God and others.

OUR BODY IS A REFLECTION OF OUR SOUL

Since our body is a reflection of our soul, what do the people around us see? Do they see a person who is totally committed to Jesus Christ and is determined to follow Him? Do they see one who is self-controlled or one driven by their desires? One who is balanced in every way or one who constantly goes to extremes? One who is as concerned with the health and well-being of their body as they are with their spirit? Do they want to be a follower of Jesus because of the example we lead and the lifestyle we live?

SINCE OUR BODY IS A REFLECTION OF OUR SOUL, WHAT DO THE PEOPLE AROUND US SEE?

When I *(Debby)* was two, my dad became a pastor in a small town in central California. It was a true hometown in every sense of the word. There were strong connections between families, businesses, and schools. It was a great place to raise a family. Although my dad was happy there, he had always dreamed of moving to the big city. So, when I was fifteen years of age, my dad decided to move us into the heart of Los Angeles so he could pastor there. I went from being the vice-president of the junior high and being on the student council as a freshman—to not knowing one person at my new high school. I went from a large and connected youth group at church to a very small youth group—it was all a shock to my teenage system!

What does a girl do with all the sadness and pain of being uprooted from everything that made her life so comfortable? She eats! I ate when I was lonely. I ate when I was sad. I ate when I was anxious about having to begin a new life. And so, I gained weight very quickly—I went from being a short skinny kid to being a short chunky kid overnight. The resulting change from my new eating habits made me even more uncomfortable in my new world—and so I ate some more!

I wasn't the only one in our family not thrilled about our move. You see, my mother was also unhappy with her own world as it was being turned upside down. This made it even more difficult for us to get along—and so I ate! And she began to nag me about my weight. We were both so obsessed with my weight gain that my mother even took me to get diet pills in a shady part of town.

I knew that "weight" was a significant thing for my mother. Even after losing all of my extra pounds as a teenager, through the years, my ears always perked up when I heard my mother speak about "weight" to other family members—and I felt their pain. Let's just say that she never learned the art of delicate diplomacy regarding this subject! My mother was a relatively private person about herself, and I did not understand the importance of this subject for many years.

When my mother was thirteen, she had to give up her education to care for the home and her younger siblings. Her mother had become confined to a wheelchair, so my mom was needed to wash clothes by hand, hang them to dry, prepare all the meals, and clean up after her entire large family. And when the family needed extra income, she did all of those things for other households. And after the tragic suicide of her sister, the care of her two young nieces and nephew also became my mother's responsibility. My mother was bright, intelligent, articulate, and an avid reader—so no one had a clue of her personal sacrifice of giving up her education at such a young age.

I didn't get an opportunity to know my grandmother, my mother's mother, very well because she passed away when I was five. After being married many years, I told my mother my only memories of Grandma were of her being confined to a wheelchair. When I asked her why I was shocked at her answer, she used a wheelchair because she was obese!

At the age of 13, my mother had suffered personal consequences due to her own mother's obesity. At age 13, my mom had to leave school and take over her mother's duties in the home. My mother felt the shame of her own mother's obesity, and she also resented it as the reason for her not completing her education. No wonder weight was such an issue to her—she knew firsthand about genetics and consequences. She understood our family had a propensity for weight gain. She knew too well the consequences that carrying too much weight has on health and lifestyle—the consequences for the one who is overweight and everyone who loves them! When she was passionate and harped on family members' excess weight, she had her reasons—she wanted to spare them! She wanted them to live long, healthy, and productive lives because she loved them!

Is "excess" permissible to God? Lot's sons-in-law, who were pledged to be married to his daughters, thought Lot was off his rocker when he warned that Sodom and Gomorrah would be destroyed—so they stayed behind. Lot's daughters fled with their father, and when his daughters realized that there were no young men in their area, they came up with a plan.

> *Come, let's get him drunk with wine, and then we will have sex with him. That way we will preserve our family line through our father.*
>
> —GENESIS 19:32, NLT

Drinking wine in *excess* got Lot in this predicament, and obviously, his daughters knew his weakness! It is hard to fool your very own family. They know your weakness. What do *we* do in excess that may also make us more vulnerable—to be tempted, weakened to sin, or not to fulfill our destiny?

In today's world, many eat in excess and have become a slave to food. This phenomenon has skyrocketed since the 1980s, and today it has peaked to the point that two-thirds of U.S. adults are now overweight or obese.[57] A study of over a million adults in the U.S. found that death rates were linked to body mass index (BMI).[58] Some researchers have determined that, in those who are highly obese, life expectancy may be reduced by an estimated 5 to 20 years.[59]

Most of us are deeply troubled by malnutrition seen around the world. We are willing to send our dollars to end this destruction of life. But what are we willing to do, when perhaps for the first time in world history, being overweight and obese are now to blame for more deaths worldwide than deaths due to malnutrition?

Where is our concern when the World Health Organization quotes statistics that "44 percent of diabetes, 23 percent of ischemic heart disease, and as much as 41 percent of certain cancers can be attributed to being overweight and obesity." This same organization estimates that 2.8 million people worldwide die each year due to being overweight or obese.[60]

Childhood obesity has been on the rise in the United States for over a decade. According to the American Heart Association, approximately one in three children and teenagers are overweight or obese.[61] What are we teaching the next generation?

Again, I quote, "We are fearfully and wonderfully made!" (Psalm 139:14) Our body has its own detection center, and it can *sense* and detect—pain, hot/cold, hunger, thirst, and even danger. Yes, our body has needs, and we are responsible for its care—water, food, rest, exercise, protection, maintenance, continual health assessment, and medical intervention. We are not left dangling or in want because when our body is alerted—we are made to *respond* to our needs.

DETECTION CENTER

Our brain is in charge of this detection center that encompasses the gastro-intestinal tract, the nervous system, the hormonal system, and more. The brain's hypothalamus is the receiver of signals and determines what needs to be done to maintain a fixed weight.

But life gets a lot more complicated when we add impulses and urges to our needs, and then we develop preferences. And life gets very complicated when we add indulgences—without restraint.

AND LIFE GETS VERY COMPLICATED WHEN WE ADD INDULGENCES—WITHOUT RESTRAINT.

It Tastes Sooo Good!

Where there is no revelation, people cast off restraint.

—PROVERBS 29:18

In his New York Times bestseller, *The End of Overeating,* David Kessler gives insight into the contributing factors why we have so little restraint in our culture regarding food. David Kessler is a pediatrician, lawyer, author, and was the Commissioner of the Food and Drug Administration—and had his own struggle with weight. His dedication page says, "To Paulette, through thick and thin."

His second chapter states, "People get fat because they eat more than people who are lean."[62] And we all go, "Duh—and I paid money for this book?" But it is not just the food that we put on our plate at mealtime—we must think about *every* bite that we take throughout the day.

Phil was working four days a week out of town. His new job description was a Clinical Psychologist for the California Prison System. (1) He had a new job (2) with lots of pressure and (3) was away from home—three contributors to stress. Stress can cause impulsive eating—and "stressed" he was! Phil only gained about ten pounds a year—but over three years, that's thirty pounds! Phil said he couldn't figure out why he was gaining weight because he wasn't eating that much. So, I suggested that he keep a log of every bite that went into his mouth. It only took two days, and he got the picture—he was eating a lot more calories than he thought.

Phil should have known better because he took over his older brother's paper route when he was nine. With his route came the benefit of having his own money. He spent money on his own clothes and baseball cards, and whatever money he had leftover, he spent on food. Every block had a designated treasure!

He recounts, "On the first block, I began with a package of brownies at the Helm's Bakery truck. And then, on the next block, I hit the Foster Freeze and got a cheeseburger, fries, and a milkshake. And then on the next street, I went to Graham's market and poured a package of peanuts into a 16 oz R.C. Cola for the ride back home."

To cap it all off, Phil would then go home to a home-cooked southern-style meal. Since Phil didn't want his mother to know about his frequent stops on his paper route, he would eat every bite on his plate. He gained weight very quickly and began becoming obese at a very young age.

At sixteen, Phil decided to do something about his weight. He went on a stringent diet and worked out at the local YMCA. And with extreme desire and discipline, he was able to shed all his excess weight. So, Phil wasn't new to the issue of weight gain. But when he was calculating his daily calories, he was still surprised by all he was consuming—because the calories added up! Kessler describes, "So much of our eating takes place outside our awareness that it's easy to underestimate how much food we actually put into our bodies."[63]

"How much we eat predicts how much we weigh."[64] Dr. Kessler also states, "Researchers have shown that what we eat doesn't depend solely on signals sent by the brain to maintain a stable weight. Another region of the brain, with different circuitry, is also involved, and often it's in charge. This is known as the 'reward system.' And in America, in the fight between energy balance and reward, the 'reward system' is winning."[65]

Our reward system has been sabotaged by the combination of sugar, fat, and salt. It is not sugar by itself that we crave, but it is when combined with fat and salt—this is why we absolutely have to have *more*, even though we don't require more calories. It tastes so good that we have turned off our hypothalamus and refuse to listen to the warning, and instead, we become a slave of our reward system. "Eating foods *high* in sugar, fat, and salt makes us eat *more* foods high in sugar, fat, and salt."[66]

OUR REWARD SYSTEM HAS BEEN SABOTAGED BY SOME COMBINATION OF SUGAR, FAT, AND SALT.

The food industry discovered this secret along *with* flavor-enhancing chemicals! An insider said that once the food industry discovered this magical combination, they became "the manipulator of the consumers' minds and desire."[67] I don't know if restaurateurs knew about the brain chemicals that are released when we experience rewarding foods or if they just saw the results. It tastes sooo good we have to have more! And before we know it, we are driving down *their* street and right into *their* parking lot!

Dr. Kessler states, "The neurons in the brain that are stimulated by taste and other properties of highly palatable food (food that tastes really good!) are part of the opioid circuitry, which is the body's primary pleasure system. The "opioids," also known as endorphins, are chemicals produced in the brain that have rewarding effects similar to drugs such as morphine and heroin. Stimulating the opioid circuitry with food drives us to eat."[68]

"Highly rewarding food becomes reinforcing because we've learned that it makes us feel better. Eventually, the actions that lead to pleasure become imprinted on the brain, and the habit of pursuit becomes firmly established."[69] "When our brain circuits have adapted to a predictable pattern of behavior, we find ourselves in a cycle of CUE – URGE – REWARD – HABIT."[70]

THOUGHTLESSLY EATING

We thoughtlessly and unintentionally eat—instead of eating with purpose and direction. We have become conditioned to eat more. We then add our emotional state, which triggers our need to feel better. I need the tastiest foods which have been sugared, oiled, and salted not to feel bored, lonely, sad, angry, anxious or stressed. These foods make us feel better, but unfortunately, it is only for the moment. The "bigger" problem is that this food has left an imprint on your brain, "creating a void that will need to be filled the next time you are cued. The result is a spiral of *wanting*."[71]

WE ARE THOUGHTLESSLY AND UNINTENTIONALLY EATING, INSTEAD OF EATING WITH PURPOSE AND DIRECTION.

For centuries mothers have been concerned about making sure their children are adequately nourished. Now, that is seemingly being superseded by ensuring young children have the latest technology. And that they are appropriately stimulated at the youngest age and select and pay for the proper pre-school and further education. Now nutrition has become an afterthought.

The highly educated mother of a two-year-old declared, "I have learned to choose my battles—and it is *not* at mealtime!" The child hops down without eating anything, and a little while later, the mother asks, "Do you want something to eat?" Knowing her child's favorites, she asks, "Do you want potato chips or Cheetos?" This mother probably has no idea that she is responsible for altering her young child's brain circuitry regarding food that they might retain for life.

Dr. Kessler stresses that the outcome of lifelong obesity is not genetic only, but lifelong obesity is environmental and avoidable.[72] I *(Debby)* have personally seen firsthand and experienced that genetics promotes the *propensity* for obesity, but it is our *choices* that will dictate the outcome!

Remember Phil's food consumption on his paper route? Well, when he turned the route over to his younger brother seven years later, he made him acquainted with both routes—the paper route, and the even more critical route, the "food" route. Needless to say, in concise order, his brother became obese as well! The re-wiring of the brain and consumption was passed on within the family. By our own example, what are we teaching our family, and how are we influencing them? That is a lot of power! It could last their lifetime!

We can learn new ways and develop healthy and positive habits—*if* we are willing and if we see a need and create a plan of action to change our lifestyle. But it will require hard work and diligence.

Dr. Kessler gives insight on how to become successful at learning to control your food consumption.

1. Set your own rules for eating in a controlled manner and maintaining a healthy weight.
2. Understand your own behavior around food and pay attention to everything you eat.
3. Seek alternative rewards that satisfy you.
4. Find support from people who care about you.
5. Bear in mind how the brain processes stimuli and how that "fix" drives your behavior in the presence of food and food cues.

6. Always be aware of what the food industry is trying to sell you and why.[73]

As Christians, do we approach our diet and lifestyle exactly like our morally upright but spiritually blinded next-door neighbor? Or do we see the necessary changes as a way to honor and worship our Holy God—laying our body and all of its appetites and preferences on the altar of sacrifice?

For our lifestyle change to become spiritual, we must embrace the leading of the Holy Spirit in our own spirit.

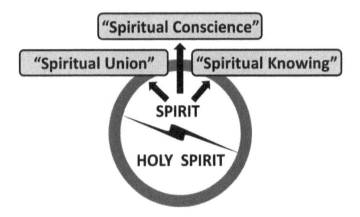

First, we must recognize that it is our spirit's "Spiritual Knowing" speaking to us—revealing that God has a more significant and better purpose for our life! And then our "Spiritual Conscience" responds, recognizing that we have not done our part! And then asking in our "Spiritual Union" with God that as we seek Him and His wisdom, He will impart to us His revelation on what needs to happen. God will give us a plan for eating and exercising, and He will grant us His grace to make it happen!

It Tastes Sooo Good!

Where there is no revelation, people cast off restraint; but blessed is the one who heeds wisdom's instruction.

—PROVERBS 29:18

WE HONOR THE BODY BECAUSE GOD HONORS THE BODY!

During the early formation of the Church, Plato was a prominent thinker of that day—having established the first institution of higher learning in the Western world. Even though he was born in 427 B.C., he is widely considered a pivotal figure in academic thinking. His Platonic teaching downgraded the body and emphasized the immortality of the soul. Many biblical traditions picked up on this Platonic influence. At times in Christian history, emphasis has been on the soul—and the body has been relegated to an insignificant position. The church has tended to devalue the physical body and stressed the immortality of the soul. However, the early historic Biblical Christian doctrine placed value on the soul *and* the body.

Jesus was born, lived, and died, was resurrected and ascended—in a human body just like ours—but He was not contaminated by sin. Christ, coming in a human body, reveals and paints a picture of the value and importance of the physical body—not just the soul. Otherwise, Jesus could have simply come as a spirit or a soul. But the New Testament writers were not only witnesses; they also clearly proclaimed the importance of the physical body of Jesus. Biblical Christianity began with placing great value on the total man—including the spirit, soul, *and* body.

On many occasions, the disciples were rightly focused on the need for food for nourishment. For example, they were concerned about the crowds when Jesus fed the five thousand, and they were also concerned about Jesus when He hadn't eaten before His time of ministry to the woman at the well. But the heart and emphasis of Jesus were on hungering and thirsting after *righteousness*—a right relationship with God. Although He was concerned about the physical need for food—as evidenced by His miraculous feeding of His crowds—He also disciplined His body through fasting, prayer, and a hunger for the will of God.

> *"My food," said Jesus, "is to do the will of Him Who sent Me and to finish His work."*
>
> —JOHN 4:34

Although food was necessary for His earthly body, His craving was not drawn to satisfying His physical flesh. Food was a means of nourishment to continue His passion for completing His mission. At the beginning of His ministry, Jesus prioritized His physical desires by creating a pathway in His natural brain. Jesus stated when the devil offered Him bread during His time of 40-day testing,

> *It is written: "Man shall not live on bread alone, but on every word that comes from the mouth of God."*
>
> —MATTHEW 4:4

In setting our priorities in life, we need to discipline our bodily appetites as Jesus did—and find fulfillment and joy in doing the will of the Father.

> *They soon forgot His works. They did not wait for His counsel, but gave in to craving in the desert, and tested God in the*

It Tastes Sooo Good!

wasteland. He gave them their request (food preference), but sent leanness into their soul.

—PSALM 106:13-14, New Heart English Bible, Brackets Added

Have you ever found yourself in front of the fridge—hungry, bored, habitually eating, or wanting to fill an empty or hurt place—and you reach for the ice cream? You may be looking for love in all the wrong places! You then say *"No!"* to that half-gallon of ice cream—that just moments before you had been convinced would make you happy and feel better! *Rejoice!* Instead of finding yourself indulging, you have just said *"Yes!"* to God's discernment, direction, and deliverance. As you close the door to your refrigerator, you light a candle in your spirit to envelop your soul and your body—and this becomes another step in your *"Happy Dance!"* Yes, that's right! *"THE Happy Dance"* right in the middle of your kitchen! Your soul and body are coming into alignment with your spirit—it is *"THE Happy Dance"* rejoicing in your newfound and God-given freedom!

Frederick Buechner stated, "A glutton is one who raids the icebox (refrigerator) for a cure for spiritual malnutrition."[74] I *(Phil)* think I just had an epiphany! Maybe that nine-year-old boy on his paper route was a love and attention-starved boy who became obese by eating for pleasure, rewarding hard work, and feeling better. And it became a habit. Was he looking for love in all the wrong places as he fed his pain because of a starved soul that was "frozen in time"?

Many hurting people, regardless of where the pain has originated or been perpetuated, over-indulge in their eating and other pleasures to feed the hurting flesh. In the meantime, God stands by—ready to heal and nourish their bruised heart that is "frozen in time!"

> YOUR RAVISHING DESIRE FOR FOOD MAY BE A SIGNAL OF MISPLACED HUNGER BECAUSE YOU ARE "FROZEN IN TIME"—AND YOU ARE LEFT UNSATISFIED AND WITH A HUNGRY AND LEAN SOUL.

If there is a "famine" in your family or marriage and everyone is malnourished, it may be that you are eating the wrong kinds of "food." Your body may need a different form of nutrition that does not come from bread alone. Your ravishing desire for food may be a signal of misplaced hunger because you are "frozen in time"—and you are left unsatisfied and with a hungry and lean soul.

But as Christians, we are to honor the body—although it is imperfect and incomplete due to the fall of man. But as a result of the death and resurrection of Christ, we have inherited a future that includes immortality of the soul and a new resurrection of our body. So, we glorify and honor God in our bodies *now*—in anticipation of the full redemption of our body—when it is totally redeemed and perfected.

VICTORIOUS LIVING— SPIRIT, SOUL, AND BODY REQUIRES THE "S" WORD THAT THE CHURCH RARELY UTTERS!

"*Self-Control*" is such an elusive concept that when Martin Seligman and his protégés at the University of Pennsylvania surveyed two million people, they ranked Self-Control at the *bottom* of their strengths in 24 diverse skills.[75]

Unfortunately, many Christians would have to agree!

*But the **fruit** of the Spirit is love, joy, peace, patience, kindness, goodness, faithfulness, gentleness and **self-control**.*
—GALATIANS 5:22, Emphasis Added

Solomon discovered that without restraint or Self-Control, we are left exposed and vulnerable to be defeated—spiritually or physically.

A man without self-control is like a city broken into and left without walls.
—PROVERBS 25:28, ESV

Where there is no revelation, people cast off restraint (no self-control); but blessed is the one who heeds wisdom's instruction.
—PROVERBS 29:18, Brackets Added

Self-Control is having a sound mind so that one can curb his own desires and impulses.[76] A self-controlled believer *wishes* to set restraints on his freedom, his desires, and passions.

A SELF-CONTROLLED BELIEVER *WISHES* TO SET RESTRAINTS ON HIS FREEDOM, HIS DESIRES, AND PASSIONS.

THE Happy Dance

WALKING IN THE FOG

I *(Debby)* had learned Self-Control about eating when I was a teenager, but I had never applied it to exercise. I only exercised when I felt like it—which was when the weather was perfect, and I didn't have anything better to do! Let's see how many days a year that would be? When we lived in Portland, Oregon, our next-door neighbors said, "It must be 80 degrees because I see Debby is outside!" They say it rains in Portland a little more than one-half of the year (188 days). It only has a *really* good chance to be 80° in July and August (8 weeks divided by 50% not raining = 4 weeks). I worked and was very busy, so that left only 2 days a week that I had a chance to walk (2 days x 4 weeks it didn't rain= 8 days). Since it rains 50% and it had to be above 80°, I would only walk 8 days a year—and that was if I didn't have anything better to do!

My own logic *knew* exercise is vital to good health, but I *chose* ease over discipline. How could I be so disciplined in my eating? I *chose* vanity over indulgence; thus, I *chose* "Self-Control" in that area.

You can only be Self-Controlled *if* you decide that it is worth it. "Self-Control" requires that you control "self"—that "self" that is carnal and self-indulgent. "Self-Control" can only happen with a decision—not only is this something that I feel is important and beneficial but something I actually *want* in my life!

I wanted to be "healthy and slender,"—but obviously, I did not want to be "healthy and exercise." I could only be Self-Controlled in the areas that I first *desired* to have Self Control. Now I don't want to insinuate that I can be Self-Controlled in all the right places by myself—I can't! I *need* the Holy Spirit's prompting and help. But if

I don't make Self-Control a priority or desire, the Holy Spirit does not bypass my human will. He is a "Helper," not a "Dictator!"

About 10 years ago, a large percentage of my friends and family were struggling with poor health or low energy levels. I was so thankful for the excellent health and vitality that God had given me—and I told Him so! His soft words back to me were spoken to my spirit as we conversed in our "Spiritual Union." God gently said, *"And you need to do your part!"* He didn't have to say another word—my "Spiritual Conscience" had been trying to get my attention for quite a while. I had found it relatively easy to ignore my own logic and Conscience, but I could not ignore God's revelation to my own spirit on this day. God had just given me a directive—and now, would I either *choose* to obey or ignore and push His words as far away from me as possible?

Of course, it had to be winter when God gave me marching orders. I wasn't sure how this whole exercise thing was going to work out for me. But the only thing I was sure about was that it definitely wasn't 80 degrees! With great hope and faith, I went shopping for a lightweight down jacket. All thoughts of having an excuse went out the window when I found a very stylish jacket on sale! Not wanting to be held accountable, I didn't tell my husband about my conversation with God. And while Phil was at work, I slipped out the door with my new down jacket ($79), wool cap ($8), and gloves ($11). Listening to God's directive—*priceless*!

On the first block, as the fog and frost hit my face, I looked up and said, "This is for You, God—I'm doing this as a sacrifice in worship. But I *really* need *Your* help!" You see, I don't handle cold well. And when it's cold outside, my exercise usually consists of reading a book by the fire.

I did not know if I could even do this, but my mandated walk became a time of "Spiritual Union" with God, and it was awesome!

My spirit was in control, requiring my soul and body to respond—it was *Victorious* Living in freezing "living color!" After walking five consecutive days, I asked Phil on the weekend if he would like to go for a walk. With a look of confusion, his answer was, "But it's not 80 degrees!" You should have seen the look of total surprise on his face when I donned my new down jacket and put on my wool cap and gloves, and said, "Let's go anyway!"

"This is for you, God"—but what God had asked of me was for my benefit! And when my exercise became part of my worship to the Lord, the Holy Spirit gave me extra fortitude to push through the discomfort. I was excited—if I could walk in the 40's—just wait until it is 80°!

God highlighted the need for exercise in this part of my life—but God was declaring I needed "Self-Control" in *every* area. I am now mindful of giving my body as a living sacrifice unto Him—this part of my life is a spiritual act and an act of worship. I see now that He was preparing me to experience *Victorious* Living—spirit, soul, and body—*every day*! He revealed to me how important our health is to Him. I desire to hear His voice, think His thoughts, say His words, and do His deeds—my ultimate desire is to hear His voice and *respond*. How can we do everything God has ordained for us to do if our bodies cannot function properly? How can we reach out and touch the world if our energy is depleted? What if I cannot complete my destiny because of poor choices and priorities?

Self-Control begins with a *desire*... and then a *decision*... and then *diligence*.

It becomes our honor to see our bodies as belonging to God. What we do with our body becomes a spiritual act—as spiritual as prayer and Bible study—it becomes our gift back to our God. It first requires a desire to honor God with our body.

SELF-CONTROL BEGINS WITH A *DESIRE*... AND THEN A *DECISION*... AND THEN *DILIGENCE*.

Our mind's logic often knows what we should be doing, but we need more than our logic. We need to add self-discipline. But we even need to add more than self-discipline—we need to draw upon the Holy Spirit's anointing and power. In our "Spiritual Union" with God, our prayer becomes, "Holy Spirit, teach me what this kind of worship means for me. Teach me how to worship You with my body."

> *And so, dear brothers and sisters, I plead with you to give your bodies (physical bodies) to God because of all He has done for you. Let them be a living and holy sacrifice—the kind He will find acceptable. This is truly the way to worship Him.*
>
> —ROMANS 12:1, NLT, Brackets Added

Yes, we have an edge on our morally upright but spiritually blinded next-door neighbor. This is because we are not just operating on our own willpower, and we are also not doing this solely for our health—but for a bigger purpose of honoring God. We are operating under the power of the Holy Spirit living right within us, giving us extra strength and influence. But this can only happen when we invite Him to partner with us each *moment* of our day. This is the way to *Victorious* Living!

> *Don't copy the behavior and customs of this world, but let God **transform** you (spirit, soul, and body) into a new person by changing the way you think (soul). Then you will learn to know God's will for you (spirit, soul, and body), which is good and pleasing and perfect.*
> —ROMANS 12:2 NLT, Brackets and Emphasis Added

This is when our body has the health, vitality, and strength to "Get up out of that chair!" and participate in *"THE Happy Dance!"* when "The Lord of the Dance" beckons.

Now offering our body as our living sacrifice has turned into a living testimony!

True *Victorious* Living requires that we are *Victorious* in our spirit, our soul, *and* our *body*! I want this to be *my* new normal!"

I am being TRANSFORMED... By Becoming a Living Sacrifice! ... Spirit, Soul, and Body!

Study Questions

1. Since your body is a reflection of your soul, what does the world around you see?

   Explain: _____

   _____

   _____

   _____

   _____

   _____

   _____

   _____

2. Does the world want to be a follower of JESUS because of your lifestyle?

   ☐ Yes   ☐ No

3. Are you conscious of what (nutritional value) and how much (volume) food you consume?

   ☐ Yes   ☐ No

THE Happy Dance

4. Has your reward system been sabotaged by some combination of sugar, fat, and salt?

   ☐ Yes   ☐ No

5. We can learn new ways and develop healthy and positive eating habits— *IF* (Mark each that is necessary)

   ☐ 1. We are willing   ☐ 2. See a need

   ☐ 3. Develop a plan of action   ☐ 4. Diligence

6. Rate yourself from 1-10 on each of the above:

   (1) I need lots of help here!

   (10) I have this one conquered!

7. The spiritual act of worshipping our GOD with our whole body begins with desiring to honor GOD this way. Are you ready for this adventure?

   ☐ Yes   ☐ No

8. To honor GOD with our body requires: (Mark each that is necessary)

   ☐ Desire

   ☐ Logic

   ☐ Self-Discipline

   ☐ Remembering to draw upon the HOLY SPIRIT'S anointing and power.

It Tastes Sooo Good!

9. Rate yourself from 1-10 on honoring God with your body:

   (1) I need lots of help here!

   (10) I have this one conquered!

10. Write your own prayer asking for GOD'S revelation on what this kind of worship means to you personally.

_____

_____

_____

_____

_____

_____

_____

_____

Chapter Nine

Choose This Day…

Gregory Bateson and his colleagues first described a double-bind theory in the 1950s.

DOUBLE-BIND

"A double-bind is an emotionally distressing dilemma in communication in which a person receives two or more conflicting messages, in which one of those messages cancels out the other. In agreeing and responding to one message, the other message is revoked. The result is you will automatically be wrong regardless of your response. The double-bind occurs when you cannot confront the inherent dilemma, and therefore can neither resolve it nor opt-out of the situation."[77]

Without understanding the cause, you are creating inner conflict and turmoil.

Double-Bind is very similar to the biblical term "Double-Mind."

> *Being a double-minded man, unstable and restless in all his ways (in everything he thinks, feels, or decides).*
> —JAMES 1:8 Amplified Bible

Double-bind, double-mind—our life becomes a mixture of spirit *and* flesh. The Apostle Paul in Romans makes it clear that these two entities are enemies to one another.

> *The mind governed by the flesh is hostile to God; it does not submit to God's law, nor can it do so.*
> —ROMANS 8:7

Our flesh is not at peace with our spirit but instead constantly wars against our bodily parts and our soul. They live in a contrary relationship with one another. The intent and message of Jesus and the Good News of the Gospel was to bring a dividing line of truth that would separate the desires of the flesh and form a new birth where the life of the Spirit would prevail. Jesus told us clearly, we *cannot* serve two masters. To be double-minded is to place our lives in a double-bind that will squeeze the life from us and prevent us from the victory that Christ has provided.

To finally bring peace, a "Double-Bind" requires a decision. Will you *choose* to believe, respond to, and live your life by your *spirit* or by your *soul*? Our *spirit* declares that I am forgiven and free! But then we remember all of our mistakes and poor choices, and our condemning voice makes us bound by our past. Am I free, or am I doomed by my mistakes? "Double-Bind!"

TO FINALLY BE AT PEACE, A DOUBLE-BIND REQUIRES A DECISION. WILL YOU *CHOOSE* TO BELIEVE, RESPOND TO, AND LIVE YOUR LIFE BY YOUR *SPIRIT* OR BY YOUR *SOUL*?

To discover that clear voice of the Holy Spirit, we need to quiet the soul and filter out our own personal preferences and opinions to hear the clear word of the Lord.

I *(Debby)* received a call from a dear friend who was experiencing a "Double-Bind." As I heard her story and began to feel her pain, I also experienced a "Double-Bind"—I was hearing two conflicting voices within me. One voice was so much louder because I felt her pain, and my counsel to her came from my own soul's very loud human wisdom. The very next day, after seeking God for His wisdom, I had to take back *all* my previous counsel. I had imparted man's soulish wisdom—but what she needed was God's spiritual direction!

A long time ago, my husband instructed me, "Don't think!" We had just experienced our first criticism in pastoral ministry. We lived in a home that belonged to the church and then had an opportunity to purchase our first home. And I was so excited! It was my very own place—to decorate or do whatever I wanted to do with my new home—without getting permission from the church board! It was such an exciting time for me. My mother arrived for a visit to help me put the finishing touches on the window treatments. That's when I heard of the accusation that we were now "worldly-minded" since we purchased a home. It would not have hurt so much had it not been that I liked and admired the people who were bringing the criticism, not to mention that they owned numerous homes of their own!

The excitement for my new home turned to pain and tears. I shared with my husband that all I could think about were those haunting words. That was when Phil imparted his "wisdom," "Well, if that is all that you can think about, then don't think!" This wisdom has served me well in reminding me not to let pain dominate my thinking or dwell on my problems. But sometimes, we need to remember to be healed and forget it and finally let it go!

God had answered our prayer and had given us a son, but now we were spending Christmas Day visiting him in prison! We had driven from California to Oregon, and it was a cold and foggy day by the Oregon coast, and there was not another car on that highway—or so we thought! And then the haunting red light appeared from out of nowhere—a law enforcement officer had just stopped us! We were already feeling very sorry for ourselves and told the officer our sad story. Somehow, he seemed sympathetic to our situation and, with a harsh warning, let us go without writing a ticket. But yes, he did follow us all the way to the prison—just to make sure we had been truthful!

Once again, I found myself crying out, "Where are you, God?" I had just fallen back into an old and familiar pattern. I was thinking with my old natural mind. What I should have been saying was, "Get behind me, Satan!" just like Jesus did when His human natural mind wanted to reject a painful experience. Jesus understood the influence the devil tries to induce when someone is in pain or has a fear or dread. Satan also understood *my* propensity to feel unloved or uncared for by my Heavenly Father when dealing with painful issues. Once again, I was pulling away from pain—I was pulling away from God's refining fire!

I WAS PULLING AWAY FROM PAIN—I WAS PULLING AWAY FROM GOD'S REFINING FIRE!

Those visits to see our son while he was in prison were some of the most painful of my life. At the same time, I came to have deep compassion for the families and loved ones that also had to enter that prison. Yes, they could leave, but do they really? No, they carry those haunting memories, the pained looks on their loved one's faces, the degrading stares by the officers in charge, the demeaning searches, and just the sense of despair that is looming in that atmosphere. It truly is overwhelming!

For almost four years during his incarceration, the pull of my natural mind was powerful. After all, the natural mind is only thinking of and consumed by one thing—*"me* and *mine!"* I would go back and forth between feeling so very sorry that my son had to experience that world and then back to being very angry that he had brought it all upon himself—and *us*!

It was during this incarceration that we truly began to understand the effects of FAS—Fetal Alcohol Syndrome—upon our son's life. Brent's federal defender asked us to write letters to the judge, letting him know about our son, hoping that something that we said would touch the judge's heart and that he would show mercy in his sentencing. I happened to mention in my letter that we believed FAS had strongly influenced Brent because we had just learned that his natural mother had battled alcoholism most of her adult life. Some pieces of our life with Brent began to make sense to us as we started a study of our own on the effects of alcohol upon a fetus' brain.

After she read my letter, Brent's tenacious federal defender requested and received an MRI on Brent's brain. The MRI was sent for reading to one of the country's leaders in the research of FAS. The findings were conclusive; there was brain damage in the frontal lobe of the brain, the effects due to alcohol damage while the brain is in early development.

Now, we finally had the "missing piece"—what had made Brent who he was and had made life such a challenge for him. We had so many regrets wishing that we had only known what we were dealing with his whole life—he was not just rebellious or strong-willed or obstinate.

This kind of brain damage causes deficiencies in brain functioning. Fetal Alcohol Syndrome individuals are unable to learn from painful experiences, and they cannot comprehend the consequences of their actions. But instead, if they do something once, their brain tells them to do it again. As a toddler, we had to put a barricade around the floor furnace because Brent couldn't associate hot with pain but was continually drawn to it and would incessantly touch it. Brent is extremely bright and intelligent, so we never dreamed he had a deficiency of any kind. Because of the effect of the prenatal brain damage, he had difficulty evaluating a situation and learning from his past experiences how to handle the problems at hand.[78]

And now, as Brent had grown, we were dealing with secondary disabilities of FAS. With maturity, the secondary disabilities become more observable by very high rates of disrupted school experiences, trouble with the law, and alcohol, and other substance abuse problems.[79]

I remember a children's song that says, "The devil is a sly old fox!" and yes, he certainly is. The enemy of our soul knew of Brent's weakness, and yes, Satan is roaming about seeking someone to devour! He seems to prey especially upon children, the weak, the abandoned, the unloved, and those in need. It is so unfair, but that is Satan's tactics! The pull of the old natural mind is even more intense in those with FAS because they have less reasoning power in times of duress.

Satan also knew where my weak and vulnerable areas were, and boy did he ever use them against me. At the same time, he knew where my husband's weaknesses were and taunted him with lies. Satan takes advantage of our times of stress, lies to us, and our old natural mind starts agreeing with him. The faulty thinking seems so familiar, and our old mind starts reacting, and we forget all the promises, all the words of our God, and we feel defeated. It is a "Double Bind" and a "Double-Mind." They perfectly describe the conflict between our spirit and our soul, and it can be a downward spiral until we come to our spiritual senses. We must make a choice!

Elijah confronted a culture of religiosity where they were enmeshed in combining the worship of Jehovah with the prevailing values of Baal worship. Elijah challenged God's people to not waver on God's principles, or they would wither with the trending philosophy of a *mixture* of serving God and the god of this world.

> *So, Ahab summoned all the people of Israel and the prophets to Mount Carmel. Then Elijah stood in front of them and said, "How much longer will you waver, hobbling between two opinions? If the Lord is God, follow Him! But if Baal is god, then follow him!" But the people were completely silent.*
>
> —1 KINGS 18:20-21

"Double-Bind!" "Double-Mind!" The people of God were being torn and split apart by two different opinions—the clear words of

God and the murky waters of their environment and culture. A choice needed to be made—a decision that would determine their destiny. Would they allow God to be their source and strength, or would they be drawn to a popular but polluted and empty lifestyle? The God Who answers by fire desires to cleanse and purify our spirit, soul, and body for His purposes—and for our life to be fulfilled. The alternate choice that we face may glitter like a diamond but turns out to only be a counterfeit—a zirconia!

DOUBLE-BIND! DOUBLE-MIND! THE PEOPLE OF GOD WERE BEING TORN AND SPLIT APART BY TWO DIFFERENT OPINIONS— THE CLEAR WORDS OF GOD AND THE MURKY WATERS OF THEIR ENVIRONMENT AND CULTURE.

There is also a psychological term, "Metacognition," which means: "think about your thinking." This is really a description of the biblical admonition of, "take captive every thought."[80] We have to stop, right in the middle of our thinking sentence, and speak God's truth to our natural mind and declare,

> *Get behind me, Satan! You are a stumbling block to me;… You do not have in mind the concerns of God, but merely human concerns.*
>
> —MARK 8:33

Get behind me, Satan! The words of science do not define us. I choose to believe the words of my Creator, and we *will* live in victory! FAS is a diagnosis—it is not a life sentence!" Although he has had to overcome many challenges, Brent has a fantastic personality, is bright and intelligent, has an incredible memory, is a great friend, is hard-working—and he is so much fun! I feel so honored and blessed by God that Brent completes our family—and he is also one of my best friends! I rejoice and have *"THE Happy Dance"* that Brent is our son!

Throughout the history of mankind, many individuals have been faced with severe handicaps, diagnoses, unbearable childhood and adult trauma (i.e., PTSD, FAS, ADHD, and Depression). But through God's mighty power, they have been able to overcome impossibilities. These are obstacles—but through God, they can be overcome! Through God, all things are possible.

ASK FOR WISDOM!

If any of you lacks wisdom, you should ask God, who gives generously to all without finding fault, and it will be given to you. But when you ask, you must believe and not doubt, because the one who doubts is like a wave of the sea, blown and tossed by the wind. That person should not expect to receive anything from the Lord. Such a person is double-minded and unstable in all they do.

—JAMES 1:5-8

One part of man, his spirit, asks for divine wisdom from God—and of course, God gives it. But now, the soul must agree by demonstrating *faith* that God will do what He has spoken. If his soul cannot agree, even if only by faith, he will be left feeling conflicted and confused. And instability will be the outcome! This is where another aspect of our mind enters the picture—it is volition—it is our own power to choose and decide.

I *(Phil)* met with a young man who holds in his hands a choice for a glorious future or the choice to abort that future. He has a Double-Mind and a Double-Bind. He wants to be a productive human being with the ability to be a good husband and father. But he is entangled and trapped in the bondage of an opioid addiction that prevents him from receiving the good gifts he longs for and having the life he dreams. He needs to find a narrow way[81] that leads to life, or he will continually stray on a wide path that provides immediate gratification but leads to destruction. His self-worth, his family, and his destiny hang in the balance. God, his Father, stands waiting patiently with love to bestow upon him great gifts, but he must prepare himself to receive from God's storehouse of blessings. This young man will be required to make a decision. Will Nathanael ever be able to experience *"THE Happy Dance"*?

THERE IS A COST!

We were young in ministry when a dynamic young couple found their way into our lives and church. One of our faithful musicians had not been at church for several weeks, so we decided to check on him at his home. Phil and I rang the doorbell, and a stranger opened the door. We asked to see Keith, and the young woman replied that he was still en route to the house. With a look of confusion, she asked, "We are just in the process of moving in—how do you know Keith?" We then discovered that the Keith we knew had moved out of that house—and another Keith was moving in! We began a conversation as perfect strangers—and ended with this couple becoming a part of our church and eventually becoming life-long friends.

Choose This Day...

One day about three years later, Keith called my husband with his "one phone call" from jail. He briefly shared why he had been arrested, and because of his shame, he asked that Phil and I explain everything to his wife, Rene. It was very painful to share with Rene that Keith had been arrested—and there was a homosexual element to that arrest. She was even more stunned than we were, but she forgave him and hoped for a new beginning. Shortly after the incident, they moved out of the area. We tried to maintain a long-distance relationship with them for years until he pushed us away, just like he had done with all his other Christian friends.

After not hearing from Rene for many years, I *(Debby)* received a call from her letting us know that Keith had passed away. Upon hearing those words, I feared for the worst—that Keith had committed suicide. Rene confirmed my worst fears by the end of the conversation—Keith had taken his own life.

Soon after that call, she came for an extended visit to our home. It only took us a little while to catch up and get back into our comfortable friendship. But it took her a very long time to share with me all the horror that she had experienced over the years in living with Keith. She had never shared this with anyone in her life but kept it bottled up within her for decades. She was "frozen in time!"

Rene finally shared, "But the underlying struggle, the huge secret struggle within our marriage, had started before we were married. As a teenager, my husband was sexually abused by his pastor. The effects of that would leave marks on him forever! He struggled with his own identity—he searched for happiness in secret alternative lifestyles. He was abusive to our children and me—physically, but even more, verbally and emotionally."

At one time, Keith had felt called to full-time ministry. But his wounds and his flesh drew him away. Now Rene understands that, of course, Keith was never happy to be in a church. There, his Conscience would come alive, and he was reminded of his failures. His guilt and condemnation were overwhelming, and he made everyone pay—even after his death, there was a price to pay. Keith went missing for five days, and with fearful and grieving hearts, his family had to enter the very dark world of sex and drugs in search of him. Finally, he was found dead in a hotel room where he had taken his own life. That was his final cost for many poor decisions. Keith's destiny could have been so very different had he made other choices and decisions along the way, but he had remained "frozen in time!"

There is a cost for every choice we make! What drives a man to decide to leave behind his ministry that he adored, his precious family, and forsake the life that God had ordained for him? Don was a gifted and talented musician and led the music ministry of one of the mega-churches in the Pacific Northwest. He had multiple creative gifts and used them in church ministry for several decades.

THERE IS A COST FOR EVERY CHOICE WE MAKE!

But one poor decision led to a poorer one, and soon he abandoned his family, ministry, and his God-centered destiny for a life in the homosexual community. After years in this lifestyle, he was diagnosed with HIV. It took this tragic news to get his attention. He finally made a very good decision to find his way back to God, who was waiting with forgiving and loving arms. With this decision, his loving and forgiving wife welcomed him back into her life and home.

We were a part of Don's life during his restoration. Don chose to humble himself to make things right, and we were honored to have him share his testimony for the first time at our church in Portland. There were many tears that day as Don shared the pain that his whole family experienced because of a series of poor choices that he had made. Yes, there is a cost for every decision and choice we make. Don was fortunate enough to find his way back to God and his family, but he passed away just a few years later from AIDS. He is in heaven, but he was taken way too soon—he wasn't able to complete the work that God had called him to do. His destiny was changed by a series of poor choices and decisions. There was a price to pay!

> *Cling to your faith in Christ and keep your conscience clear. For some people have deliberately violated their consciences; as a result, their faith has been shipwrecked.*
>
> —I TIMOTHY 1:19 NLT

Something in the hearts of Don and Keith pushed them to go against their own innate knowledge of the truth, bypass their own Conscience, as well as the direction of the Holy Spirit. It was their very own carnal flesh refusing to be crucified! Both of these men had a call from God for ministry but could not fulfill their destiny because of their own choices and decisions. Both of their decisions dramatically impacted their world and eventually ended both of their lives.

The difference between these two stories is the ending. One man—he found his way back to salvation through the grace of God. The other man—was found alone and dead in a motel room.

I wonder what the *first* poor decision that led to the *next* poor decision that took each one down the path of destruction was. And oh, the pain that their choices brought upon their families!

Since every choice has a cost—is it worth the price? What choices are we making today that could shorten our life or decrease the quality of the life that God has given?

Should we take more time and care in our relationships?

Should we apply healthy habits to our lifestyle?

Should we adjust our schedule?

Should we modify our diet?

In short, we must silence our flesh and listen and respond to the Holy Spirit living within us! But too often, we get saved and then slip back into old comfortable and familiar patterns of thought and behavior. We are saved from sin, but we are not delivered from our selfish nature. This is a process—a very long process. Salvation takes one decision and one second; *Transformation* (crucifying the flesh) takes many decisions over a lifetime! It only takes one *good* decision that leads to another *good* decision that leads to life! It is never too late!

SALVATION TAKES ONE DECISION AND ONE SECOND; TRANSFORMATION (CRUCIFYING THE FLESH) TAKES MANY DECISIONS OVER A LIFETIME!

"THE HAPPY DANCE" IN THE MIDST OF TRIALS?

Is it possible to have *"THE Happy Dance"* in the midst of trials? As I pondered this, my mind quickly went to Janelle, a young woman I mentored.

In the early stages of our relationship, Janelle had discovered her husband's secret stash of heroin in the attic of their garage. She had suspected for some time that something was going on with her husband, Nathanael. And the proof was there right before her very own eyes. Janelle called me, and we discussed options on how to handle this situation. We concluded that it was time for a family intervention. I called Phil at work, and Janelle reached out to all of Nathanael's immediate family, and with everyone on board, we decided to meet that night.

Once Janelle knew that Nathanael had brought drugs into the sanctuary of their home, everything had changed. With his toddler sitting in the walker at his feet, and his very young son sitting in his lap with his arm around his daddy's neck, Nathanael was presented with an ultimatum—go to drug rehab or move out of the home. At first, there was resistance and then came the tears as the severity of the situation sunk in. Because of Nathanael's tremendous love for his family, he consented and chose to go to a Christian-based live-in treatment program called Teen Challenge. We were so proud of Janelle as she used so much self-control and lovingly communicated with her husband that evening. We were so proud of Nathanael as he was willing to make a life-changing decision and consented to leave his family and the area for a 12-month program. What a sacrifice for them all!

Over that year, Janelle was faced with many obstacles that she had never experienced before. About two years earlier, she had given up a lucrative and influential career—she felt God had called her to be home with her young family as her primary focus. Now at this time, the family was in financial disarray because of Nathanael's drug-focused lifestyle. His business was not bringing in income but had even become a stressful and financial liability. They had the very real potential of losing their home.

Janelle could have easily picked up her old job again, but she felt God impressing her that He wanted to be her source for everything. What a Double-Bind! The question was—would she say *I* can figure life out and *I* can make this work? Or would she learn to rely on God like she never had before? Would she choose *her* own way or God's way?

From where I'm standing, I see a very talented and capable young woman who is also one of the most spiritually hungry women I have ever known. My natural woman would say to her, "Girl, go get your great career back and bring security and prosperity back to your household." But I didn't say a word during this process because I *knew* that she was seeking God—continually—and He kept giving her the same answer.

Over the following months, Janelle put her faith in God into practice. She began posting anointed worship videos proclaiming her love and adoration of God through music. As people started to watch these videos, many were overwhelmed and blessed. Her Holy Spirit-infused spirit was in control—she silenced her selfish and emotional soul and kept her eyes upon God.

Most people didn't know her burden—they just felt her love and faith in her God! She was "free"—free to worship, free to minister to God and to her world! She was so free of her soul's influence—she was free to *continually* maintain *"THE Happy Dance!"* She allowed the Holy Spirit to permeate her spirit, and her spirit became strong enough to say to her soul—look at the *goodness* of the Lord—let's celebrate the "Lord of the Dance!" Janelle's *"Happy Dance"* was possible because she did not give in to "self," even in the worst of circumstances.

SHE WAS SO FREE OF HER SOUL'S INFLUENCE—SHE WAS FREE TO *CONTINUALLY* MAINTAIN "THE HAPPY DANCE!"

Because of her spirit, soul, and body coming into alignment with God, she *maintained "THE Happy Dance!"* And she was still smiling and trusting God even when she *did* lose her home, even when she didn't know where she and her family would live. This *"Happy Dance"* was not a dance of *celebration* but a *"Happy Dance"* inspired by *trust!*

God had spoken, Janelle received and believed, and God delivered like only she knew He would! She knew God would come through! God did the miraculous and provided a rent-free home to her. The amazing part was that it was provided by someone who did not know of her situation but did so because God had impressed it upon their heart.

Janelle was having *"THE Happy Dance!"* But the point is, she was having that *"Happy Dance"* long before she was even provided a place to live. This *"Happy Dance"* started in the midst of her turmoil and never wavered.

As I observed how Janelle was handling "life," this mentor was being taught by her mentee! Yes, you can maintain *"THE Happy Dance!"* and be *Victorious* in the *midst* of trials. But to do this, you must choose to control your own "self" and allow your spirit to rule!

We are all so proud of Nathanael that he did the hard work and chose to allow for his soul to be *transformed* during the twelve months of being away from his family. He chose to put God and

THE Happy Dance

his family first, and during this process, he and Janelle learned to control "self" at the exact time. You can only imagine the joy they felt when Nathanael completed rehab and re-joined his family in absolute surrender to God! This *"Happy Dance!"* was with the "Lord of the Dance"— *and* Nathanael!

Even good and right choices have a cost. There is a cost—but it is so worth the price! Applying God's wisdom and crucifying the flesh is so worth the price—the rewards are righteousness, peace, and joy—it is real life! It is *Victorious* Living—spirit, soul, and body!

Choose this day. Will you serve your own soul and body? Or will you crucify the flesh and make the right decisions that contribute to *Victorious* Living—in your spirit, soul, and body?

The right decisions create an atmosphere for *"THE Happy Dance!"*

I am being TRANSFORMED... *By Making Godly Decisions!*

Study Questions

1. Re-read the definition for "Double-bind". Have you faced a Double-bind in your past?

   ☐ Yes ☐ No

   Are you experiencing one currently?

   Explain: _____

   _____

   _____

   _____

   _____

2. What decision do you need to make to resolve your Double-bind/Double-mind?

   Explain: _____

   _____

   _____

   _____

   _____

3. Are you going through a current trial or testing?

   ☐ Yes   ☐ No

   What makes it most challenging?

   Explain: _____

   _____

   _____

   _____

   _____

4. What is your plan to be able to walk through this trial?

   Explain: _____

   _____

   _____

   _____

   _____

5. Place a check mark beside each that will be involved.

   ☐ Choose and learn how to really trust GOD

   ☐ Not judging Him

   ☐ Not trying to understand "why"

   ☐ Putting aside your natural logic

6. What source do you seek when you need wisdom?

   ☐ Mentor   ☐ Nosey Neighbor

   ☐ Gossipping Gertrude   ☐ Small Group

   ☐ Time with GOD   ☐ Trusted Friend

   ☐ The Bible

7. Do you take the time to count the cost for each choice that you make daily?

   ☐ Yes   ☐ No

8. This chapter is filled with stories of people and their choices. What kind of choices are you making today that will change your life—for good, or that will lead to future pain?

   Explain: _____

   _____

   _____

   _____

9. Since every choice has a cost—is it worth the price? What choices are you making today that could shorten your life, or the quality of the life that GOD has given?

   _____

   _____

   _____

   _____

10. Should you apply healthy habits into your lifestyle?

    ☐ Yes   ☐ No

    What is your plan?

    Explain: _____

    _____

    _____

    _____

11. Should you take more time and care in your relationships?

    ☐ Yes   ☐ No

    What is your plan?

    Explain: _____

    _____

    _____

    _____

12. Should you modify your schedule?

    ☐ Yes   ☐ No

    What will be your plan to make it happen?

    Explain: _____

    _____

    _____

    _____

Chapter Ten

Who Holds the Deed?

Stewardship is the one "S" word that we *do* regularly hear in church! But often, Stewardship has been relegated to just giving to the church with our tithes and offerings or to the new building campaign—but Stewardship is so much more!

OWNERSHIP

The path of Stewardship begins in Genesis.

> *In the beginning God created the heavens and the earth.*
>
> —GENESIS 1:1

And as the Creator of all things, He really has absolute "ownership" of all things. This premise is the foundation for Biblical Stewardship. But this knowledge of God's ownership must pass from my understanding and grasping its meaning ("Comprehend")—to recognizing God's ownership as important to me ("Apprehend")—and then to fervently agree that God's ownership is truth to me ("Embrace"). But many Christians stop at this point in the revelation—having gained head and heart knowledge of this truth, without putting Stewardship into practice ("Apply").

Stewardship begins with recognizing God's ownership of your life and embracing that premise. The next step is to have a desire and a willingness to submit to Him. Our culture screams, "Don't tell me what to do—you're not the boss of me!" Oh, but yes, He is! The Bible says,

> *The earth is the Lord's, and everything in it, the world, and all who live in it.*
>
> —PSALM 24:1

The foundation of Stewardship recognizes that as Creator, God has ownership of you and everything around you. It is from this fundamental truth that Stewardship is understood. He is the Creator and owner—you are His manager!

A steward is somebody who manages someone else's property, finances, or household. And by guidance and direction, bring a project to completion.[82]

Biblical Stewardship means:

- Everything that we are: our identity, our character, our reputation, our talents, and abilities...
- Everything that we manage: our resources, our time, our energy, our environment, our marriage/relationships, our health, and our ministry...

- Our total sum... Everything that we are... everything that we own and manage is given back to God—because He is the rightful owner!

For we are co-workers in God's service; you are God's field, God's building.

—1 CORINTHIANS 3:9

EVERYTHING THAT WE ARE, EVERYTHING THAT WE OWN AND MANAGE, IS GIVEN BACK TO GOD— BECAUSE HE IS THE RIGHTFUL OWNER!

"You are God's field" implies that you are "cultivated"—meaning you are not hardened by your own "self" interest but have allowed God to break up the soil of your heart so that you are able to receive His instruction and guidance.

"You are God's building"— You are the very home of God!

God has called us to be His *"co-workers."* Thus, God's purpose becomes our purpose. God's purpose is He wants to redeem the world, and Stewardship defines how our life helps make this purpose possible.

OWNER'S MANUAL

You do not belong to yourself, *for God bought you with a high price.*

—1 CORINTHIANS 6:19-20 NLT, Emphasis Added

Stewardship is not God taking something from us—it is His means of bestowing His richest gifts upon His children. His law, statutes, precepts, commands, and decrees are His gifts given *for* our benefit and blessing—these are the means to help us become a faithful steward of His creation.

Proper Stewardship is one of the gifts of grace upon our life. His grace and our Stewardship combined enable us to become what we were created to be and to fulfill our destiny upon this earth! Our own spirit recognizes this as truth—but sometimes, our soul and body are harder to convince!

> *Do not let any part of your body become an instrument of evil to serve sin. Instead,* **give yourselves completely** *to God, for you were dead, but now you have new life. So, use your whole body as an instrument (Stewardship) to do what is right* **for the glory of God.**
>
> —ROMANS 6:13, Brackets and Emphasis Added

One generation lived by rules, and they were able to check them off to feel religious and righteous. But observers realized that most of those regulations were man-induced and were not what God had in mind. So, the next generation threw out *all* the rules. Observers realized that was not what God had in mind either. With this profound insight, maybe *this* generation will actually go to God and His Word for *His* holy and specific direction. Maybe this generation will come to understand that God's mandates are really His love mandate. We find the joy of *"THE Happy Dance"* irresistible. But there is also joy in being a good steward of God's temple—you! Stewardship requires responsibility and accountability, but there is also a reward—it is the joy of having our God's approval.

OUR LIFE BELONGS TO GOD!

We had traveled to a conference and were at the airport waiting for our flight home. And then we both saw him—a young man who looked *exactly* like our son. We both stopped, stared, and wanted to take his picture—but we put the camera away and tried to stop staring. For years this has become a pattern. Whenever we see someone who looks exactly like him, we feel compelled to stop and to intercede for whatever is happening at that moment. Yes, it is troubling, but we feel honored and touched that God cares enough about our son that He alerts us to pray.

We planned a trip to just hang out in Jerusalem. No group, no tour—just us and Jerusalem. We had been there several times before but always in a group setting. It doesn't matter if one is leading a group or following in a group; there is never enough time just to stroll and interact with the locals—or just take time to hear God's voice. We left the States with anticipation of a holy and "Spiritual Union" with God. We went to Jerusalem seeking God—and He met us there every day!

WE LEFT WITH ANTICIPATION OF A HOLY AND "SPIRITUAL UNION" WITH GOD. WE WENT TO JERUSALEM SEEKING GOD—AND HE MET US THERE EVERY DAY!

On Mother's Day, we were drawn to Christ's Church, the oldest Protestant Church in the middle east, located right inside the ancient walled city. I *(Debby)* enjoyed interacting with a local member of the congregation; the presence of God was strong during the beautiful worship, the liturgy was anointed, and the guest speaker was fantastic.

And then it happened right before our eyes! The Jewish speaker metamorphosed into "Brent." On this day, though, when we "saw Brent," it was different—the Lord was not drawing us to intercede! On this day, we saw Brent in a *transformed* state. And on this day, we couldn't wipe the smile from our faces.

And when we left the church that morning, the streets were flooded with 60,000 young Jewish men celebrating "Jerusalem Day!" They were celebrating and singing and literally dancing down the streets! Phil and I looked at each other and said—it's *"The Happy Dance!"* I have a picture of Phil joining with those young Jewish men and doing his own *"Happy Dance"* because of the joy and freedom God had just bestowed upon him. God had allowed us to see a visual picture of the culmination of God's plan for our son.

Because we did not want to be distracted during our trip, we had kept our phones off during the entire trip. While on the shuttle drive from Los Angeles International Airport to our car, I turned on my phone, and there was a message from Brent. We had not heard from him for months, and sadly his text message to me was an apparent suicide note.

I immediately panicked, but my mind calmed as I was drawn to the image of "Seeing Brent" in Jerusalem. I again felt the hope and faith in my God that I had sensed that day. I did not shed a tear—I did not make a frantic call—I immediately gave it all to God.

Nine days later, after months of no contact, Brent called us, and within a week, he came for a ten-day visit. We knew God had been up to something!

Who Holds the Deed?

We were watching the news together in our living room when they announced that the second celebrity, within a few days, had committed suicide. Since Brent had arrived, we had not breached the subject of his last text message. Brent has struggled with thoughts of suicide for many years, but our family has always seen it from different perspectives. Several times Phil and I had been on the end of trying to help family members and friends put their own lives back together after a loved one's suicide. We both felt that it was selfish for someone to leave loved ones here on earth to deal with the loss. But our son felt that it was selfish to ask someone to live and have to face the kind of pain that would cause them to want to take their own life.

This day while watching the news deliver the tragedy of yet another suicide, Brent put his hand up and declared, "Stop! I know what you are going to say! You don't have to—I've had an epiphany!" And then he told his story, "Just after I said good-bye to all my friends and wrote you that message, I took off on foot and ended up at a school. It was a Sunday, so there was no one else around. When the gravity of what I was about to do became so real, I suddenly sat on the concrete. While sitting there, I somehow fell into a deep sleep. When I woke up, I had my answer. God revealed to me that the very thing that brought us life at creation was when God breathed the Holy Spirit into us. God also revealed to me that suicide was not His will. At first, I got mad at God for taking away my plan. But then I accepted it." God knew exactly how to share His heart with Brent.

The devil, our adversary, the liar to humanity, the deceiver of Christians, the thief—has his own plan. This plan is to kill and destroy lives. That is his full-time job! He is self-employed, very diligent, and very motivated. Using the negative triad of fear, pain, and shame—the devil's plan is to instill lies and deception—hoping that he can etch them into the hearts and minds of individuals to keep them "frozen in time."

The devil convinces them that their life is so painful and not worth living. He convinces them to take their own life into their hands and destroy it. They do not want to die—they just want to kill the pain!

USING THE NEGATIVE TRIAD OF FEAR, PAIN, AND SHAME—THE DEVIL'S PLAN IS TO INSTILL LIES AND DECEPTION—HOPING THAT HE CAN ETCH THEM INTO THE HEARTS AND MINDS OF INDIVIDUALS TO KEEP THEM "FROZEN IN TIME."

When it reaches that point, Satan takes the deception and burden and multiplies it—as the negative triad is then transferred upon the backs, minds, and hearts of their family and loved ones. Their survivors now carry that burden, plus the burdens of guilt and remorse—just like my own mother had experienced with her sister's suicide. Do you see how crafty and insidious the devil is?

This is even happening in elementary schools and in churches—two places you would never think possible. What is happening in our culture? This month alone, we have personally heard of a dynamic leader from a church we attended as well as another pastor in our state—both committing suicide.

We do not fully understand all the details of these events—nor do we wish to make any personal judgments. And we don't minimize their pain! But we are burdened and concerned about the vulnerable and hurting people of our world, who may not understand God's value and timing of life. With all of the good words spoken, was anyone brave enough to address the magnitude and ramifications of the tragedy of suicide? By our silence, can the devil lie and say that the church is condoning suicide and that we are somehow giving permission for this method of escaping life's problems and difficulties? Like our culture, are we just trying to smile so we can somehow move on?

As our son was getting ready to return home after his visit, I asked him, "What day was it that God spoke to you, and you had your 'epiphany' about suicide." With his head down, he said, "It was on Mother's Day." While Phil and I were back in Jerusalem smiling and having a *"Happy Dance,"* —Jesus, the Great Intercessor, was hard at work!

We don't know who is reading this book. If you have kids prone to depression or suicide, let our story encourage you about the power of your prayers. If you have dealt with suicide personally, don't let the devil, our adversary, heap condemnation or guilt or shame upon you. Tell the devil, whenever he tries to point his accusing finger at you, to leave your presence because you are not listening to his lies any longer! Shake the accusing dust off of yourself in your shallow grave and jump for joy as you are free—free enough to experience *"THE Happy Dance!"*

EVERYTHING WE ARE BELONGS TO GOD

Everything that we are: our character, our identity, our reputation, our talents, and abilities—really belong to God!

Character begins inwardly—in the heart and mind, and then is demonstrated outwardly—for all to see. Character defines us. It impacts our identity, our reputation, and our talents and abilities. In reality, our character is our testimony to the world!

The old adage is: Your character is who you are when no one else is looking.

Merriam Webster describes character as the mental and ethical traits marking and often individualizing a person.

While sitting in Chapel in my *(Phil)* freshman year of college, with a myriad of things running through my mind—such as the girls sitting across the aisle—my attention was drawn back to a dignified, older, white-haired man who was eloquently speaking from the pulpit. The words that penetrated my heart from John W. Follet were these, "Someday when you stand before the judgment seat, what is important will be, not how many great feats you have accomplished, but how much you have been conformed to the image of Christ!" I thought, wow, I should probably work more on my character and not just my ambitions.

For God knew His people in advance, and He chose them to **become** *like His Son...*

—ROMANS 8:29, Emphasis Added

Dallas Willard states, "The *transformation* of our thought life by taking on the mind of Christ—His ideas, images, information, and patterns of thinking—opens the way to deliverance of every dimension of the human self from the oppressing powers of darkness."[83]

Love for others should be the foundational characteristic for all to see! Saul, who was "frozen in time" until his Damascus experience, was *transformed* and became Paul—replacing the negative triad of fear, shame, and pain—with faith, hope, and love.

C. S. Lewis borrows a parable from George McDonald and articulates, "Imagine yourself as a living house. God comes to re-build that house. At first, perhaps, you can understand what He is doing. He is getting the drains right and stopping the leaks in the roof and so on; you knew that those jobs needed doing, and so you are not surprised. But presently, He starts knocking the house about in a way that hurts abominably and does not seem to make any sense. What on earth is He up to? The explanation is that He is building quite a different house from the one you thought of—throwing out a new wing here, putting on an extra floor there, running up towers, making courtyards. You thought you were being made into a decent little cottage: but He is building a palace. He intends to come and live in it Himself."[84]

EVERYTHING WE HAVE BELONGS TO GOD!

Phil was 23, and I was 20 when God changed our ministerial emphasis from youth ministry to leading a very small congregation in a little mountain town. The salary was minimal, and there were no jobs for me. In addition to church ministry, Phil was able to substitute teach at both the middle school and high school. We were definitely living paycheck to paycheck, and there was never anything left over to pay our tithe to God. It was time for us to put into practice the following principle,

> *A tithe of everything from the land, whether grain from the soil or fruit from the trees, belongs to the Lord; it is holy to the Lord.*
>
> —LEVITICUS 27:30

Phil had learned to tithe at an early age on the income he received from his paper route. This came about when his Sunday school teacher, Mack Alford, painted on a wall these words, "Will a man rob God?"

THE Happy Dance

It made an impression on a nine-year-old boy, and from that point forward, Phil made tithing his priority. Since our resources belonged to God, the Holy Spirit brought conviction upon Phil, and he declared, "We are going to start giving God His tithe *before* we pay a single bill." It had become our practice to pay our tithe as a bill. But from this point on, we were going to give to God what was His *first*. Of course, ever since that day, as we put God first in our finances—there is always just *enough*. We have seen Him stretch the remainder and even send us checks in the mail!

My dear friend, Rene, had lost her husband when he tragically committed suicide. Shortly after his suicide, things for her took a turn for the worse. She lost her job, her home, and to add even more burden; she was diagnosed with cancer! Rene knew that I had a business degree, and right during her financial tsunami, she asked me for some advice. She came to visit for a few days, and the plan was we were going to make a budget for her new life. Her sole source of income now was social security, and she was having difficulty living within her means.

When I put her income and expenses onto a spreadsheet, I was mortified—there was not enough to live on, much less give God His tithe! I was saddened and discouraged. I asked Phil to put on his pastor's hat, and then I explained to him that Rene did not have enough to buy groceries—much less to pay her tithe. Would he advise her to give God His tithe *first*? Would his advice be the same for this precious widow as it had been for countless others during his entire ministry? We began to share with Rene the principles of God's blessing on those who tithe. Rene and her late husband had never made a habit of tithing and, therefore, had never experienced the joy of God's full blessing. We read together,

Who Holds the Deed?

Will a mere mortal rob God? Yet you rob Me. But you ask, "How are we robbing You?" In tithes and offerings.

—MALACHI 3:8

It was a fresh and glorious time together as we sat in God's presence. When this teaching from Malachi became so alive and brought tears to all of our eyes, we felt God challenging us to put His Word to the test. Phil made a deal with Rene: if she was willing to tithe *first* from her small income for three months, and *if* God didn't provide *enough* for her groceries and other needs, Phil and I would pay her back every penny of her tithe. Rene agreed to the deal, and needless to say, we were all anxious to see if God would be as faithful to Rene as He had been to us.

WE FELT GOD CHALLENGING US TO PUT HIS WORD TO THE TEST.

God gave us inspiration and ideas for additional income. Rene has a servant's heart, and it is her joy to help people. So, we thought, why not turn that into a business of driving senior citizens to appointments and help with shopping! A business card was designed, we thought of ideas on advertising her new business, and she was off and running. We even prayed for God to send checks in the mail!

God has proven His faithfulness time and time again to Rene! Her business has flourished by referrals. He has sent unexpected checks in the mail—and God even provided an expense-free trip to

Hawaii! Yes, He's a good, good Father! In the midst of all this, Rene even earned extra income by renting out her spare bedroom. God loves to bless someone who is willing to do their part and be a good Steward of their own time, energy, and resources. By the way, if you're wondering, Phil never had to repay Rene for her tithes—not one penny—there was always just *enough*!

But for Rene to get to this place, she had to take a journey—a journey of taking steps not to remain "frozen in time." The Sunday after Keith's suicide, Rene made her way back to church. She was in a world of hurt and knew where she had to go to find her answers. She took her own negative triad of fear, shame, and pain with her shock and grief.

Sometime later, God began redeeming Rene's pain and loneliness when she looked around the church and reflected, there must be women, just like me, that need encouragement and fellowship to get through the lonely and dark times. God impressed upon Rene's pastor that she should start "Solo Ministry"—a ministry directed to single women. It has become so effective that other churches in the Sacramento area have also included "Solo Ministry" into their churches. The denomination of the church that she attends has just asked permission for "Solo Ministry" to be used district-wide. God is the Redeemer and Restorer of lives.

TRUSTWORTHY

We have had a property for years that we could never sell. We understood that had been by God's design when we moved back into the home when Phil was finishing his doctorate. Then when Phil was transferred to a position in another community, we put it up for sale. It was a real estate slump once again, and we could not sell it. Yet again, we trusted God with the home that He had provided and that we loved.

God always sent the best tenants—we knew this was His favor and grace! The tenants during that time took such good care of our property that our handyman and our gardener were both in awe that they were taking care of our property as if they owned it. They even had their two sets of twins take their shoes off to protect the new flooring! They were good Christians and good stewards of property that was not their own—and it became a testimony!

After four years of renting from us, we received a call from our tenants, and they made an offer to buy our home. God honored them, and the rental they had been taking such good care of became their own! God blessed them—God blessed us—and God was honored throughout the whole transaction. God was present in every detail—God honored two families who desired to properly manage His resources and make Him the Owner of their lives!

And if you have not been trustworthy with someone else's property, who will give you property of your own?

—LUKE 16:12

IT'S NEVER TOO LATE!

When God gives new Revelation, many Christians will declare, "Oh no! I didn't know what I was doing! I didn't see it as my 'spiritual' responsibility!" "I feel so much regret!"

They speak about a lack of knowledge, understanding, or wisdom regarding their responsibility to Godly Stewardship. Our own flesh and the enemy of our soul will want to use this teaching

THE Happy Dance

on Stewardship to heap condemnation upon us for not managing our resources well—whether it is our physical body, or our soul's emotions and desires, or our finances. Yes, our God brings conviction, and He desires that we make way for change, but He does so with tremendous compassion and understanding. We need to ask God for His forgiveness—but we must also forgive ourselves. If we don't forgive ourselves, regret will turn into condemnation.

THERE IS GOOD NEWS—IT IS NEVER TOO LATE TO BEGIN TO PROPERLY STEWARD GOD'S TEMPLE.

There is good news—it is never too late to begin to properly steward God's temple. God always compensates for our efforts, no matter how late we arrive to suit up in the game! I think that Jesus' parable of the workers in the vineyard shows us His grace.

> *"These who were hired last worked only one hour," they said, "and you have made them equal to us who have borne the burden of the work and the heat of the day."*
>
> —MATTHEW 20:12

God is a restorer of His creations. God restores the years that our flesh and even the devil dominated our temple.

> *I will restore to you the years that the swarming locust has eaten...*
>
> —JOEL 2:25

This is a picture of how our God desires and can restore our bodies, emotions, relationships, and our worship of God.

> *The master was full of praise. "Well done, my good and faithful servant. You have been faithful in handling this small amount, so now I will give you many more responsibilities. Let's **celebrate** together!"*
> —MATTHEW 25:21, NLT, Emphasis Added

Yes! It's *"THE Happy Dance!"* Because you have learned Stewardship, this is an *approval celebration*—it is an invitation to celebrate *with* "The Lord of the Dance" as *He* is celebrating *you!*

I am being TRANSFORMED...
By Being a Good Steward...
I Am Serving the Creator, Instead of the Creature!

Study Questions

1. What Stewardship changes are necessary for you to move into action?

    ☐ Desire   ☐ Practical Steps

    ☐ Discipline   ☐ Time and Energy

    ☐ Determination   ☐ Follow Through

2. We are to Steward everything as He directs, because they ultimately belong to GOD. Our own strength is not enough! What areas must you learn to rely more on the HOLY SPIRIT?

    ☐ Home   ☐ Belongings and Possessions

    ☐ Time   ☐ Budget and Investments

    ☐ Energy   ☐ Natural Resources

    ☐ Money

3. Are you more prone to:

    ☐ Adhere to man-made mandates   OR   ☐ Throw off all mandates

How does this impact God's mandates?

Explain: _____

_____

_____

_____

_____

_____

4. Stewardship reflects our value of the item we are overseeing. What do you see when you look in the mirror? If you are like most people, are you drawn to see your flaws?

Explain: _____

_____

_____

_____

_____

_____

5. Have you ever had suicidal thoughts?

☐ Yes ☐ No

Do you need a better understanding of God's value on your life?

☐ Yes ☐ No

Can you identify the emotional pain that prompts those negative triad thoughts of fear, pain, and shame?

☐ Yes   ☐ No

Explain: _____

_____

_____

_____

_____

_____

6. Character begins in the heart and mind and then is demonstrated for all to see. Is your character a testimony of God's redemption and *transformation*?

   ☐ Yes   ☐ No

7. Would God be pleased with how you spend your time, energy, and money?

   ☐ Yes   ☐ No

8. Does your management style need a *transformation*?

   ☐ Yes   ☐ No

9. Have you discovered the blessing and made tithing a practice?

   ☐ Yes   ☐ No

10. What adjustments are necessary to keep tithing a priority?

    Explain: _____

    _____
    _____
    _____
    _____
    _____
    _____
    _____

Chapter Eleven

A Day of Delight... A Fresh Beginning!

"TIME TO PICK UP YOUR PACE!"

My God-mandated walk is now the most incredible part of my day. God has transformed this "I *(Debby)* don't even *want* to walk" non-walker into—I can't wait to get out the door walker (on most days!). My walks have become the special times of "Spiritual Union" with my God. I talk—He talks! And when He speaks, it consumes my soul—because it is His fresh revelation to my own spirit. I come home refreshed, renewed, and ready to get to work—physically and spiritually.

At the halfway point during one of these walks, I noticed a very fast-walking couple. And the thought popped into my mind, "I want to walk like *that*! God must have read my mind because His response was, *"Okay, Debby, it's time to pick up your pace!"* Because I know how much God cares about me, I knew that He was speaking physically. I knew that God was addressing the cardio aspect of my walking. Now I am not a sloooow walker, but neither am I a fast walker. With the couple ahead of me, it became my challenge that day to keep pace with them. And I did—all the way home! That day I received a new mandate from God!

The next day I began to incorporate God's new plan into our daily walk together. I could take my time on the first half, but the last half—yes, you got it—I was to "pick up the pace." Observation: It is easier to keep focused when following the right example. Without the couple ahead of me to keep me on pace, I would get distracted. I would observe a roadrunner crossing my path—my attention would wander to a lovely plant—I would notice the landscapers keeping everything beautiful—and I would slow my pace with these distractions. And I got it! If this happens physically, I *know* it happens spiritually!

Since we live by the Spirit, let us keep in step with the Spirit.
—GALATIANS 5:25

What was God saying, and what was God doing? That I was to keep my spiritual eyes on Him so that I can follow at His pace—without any distractions! I believe God is saying to His church, *"Okay, Church, it's time to pick up your pace* and *keep your eyes on Me—we've got much to do!"*

After my fast-paced walks, I can hardly wait to get into my cool house (remember, I live in the desert!) and put my feet up with a cold refreshing bottle of water. From over-worked and over-heated to cool and refreshed! This is the purpose of our Sabbath Rest—because we have much to do!

If Jesus had to get away to rest because… His physical body was exhausted, His emotions were depleted, and His spirit needed

A Day of Delight... A Fresh Beginning!

refreshing—how much more do we, as fallen human beings, have the need for Sabbath Rest.

> *This High Priest of ours understands our weaknesses, for He faced all of the same testings we do, yet He did not sin.*
>
> —HEBREWS 4:15, NLT

We need a Sabbath to... Re-fresh, Re-new, and Re-focus. When we observe a Sabbath, our whole being is Re-stored—spirit, soul, body! You are restored so you can face your world, your challenges, your ministry, and your destiny!

WE NEED A SABBATH TO RE-FRESH, RE-NEW, RE-FOCUS. WHEN WE OBSERVE A SABBATH, OUR WHOLE BEING IS RE-STORED—SPIRIT, SOUL, AND BODY!

In a world with so many gadgets and items to save time and get more done, we see many who have difficulty understanding and participating in a Sabbath Rest. Many people today are restless and take a pill to sleep and then take a different pill to stay awake. For many of us, we feel guilty if we *do* rest because we believe we should be accomplishing so much more.

Why would we, as 21st-century believers, ever want to incorporate the Sabbath Rest into our lifestyle? Didn't we get away from those legalistic principles decades ago—so that we could do whatever we wish to on Sunday! Isn't the Sabbath part of the law that Jesus gave us freedom from?

What we can't do is forget that the Sabbath Rest was blessed by God long before He gave the Law to Moses! It is vitally important that we understand the "principle" of the Sabbath and not the "legalistic" interpretation of the Sabbath that the early religious leaders so fervently tried to enforce. They perverted the Sabbath and created a religion of bondage, whereas Jesus honored the Sabbath as an opportunity for rest and healing.

The importance of the Sabbath is not about a day of the week—Saturday or Sunday—but the intent of the Creator to establish health and rest for His people. The Sabbath that I want is the one promised by Jesus, to release the yoke of bondage of my heavy and weary heart and receive His light and easy yoke of freedom!

WHEN GOD SAYS "REMEMBER"... WE SHOULD NOT "FORGET"!

"Remember" is a word in the Bible that becomes a pillar of wisdom, stability, and continuity in the lives of Biblical believers. *"Remember the Passover," "Do this in remembrance of Me,"* and *"Remember the Sabbath!"* God uses "remember" to etch into our hearts, as He engraved in all Creation, an immutable truth. *"The Sabbath was made for man."* You need a break before *you* break!

After God had created all things, He looked over His creation and said it was very good! And then in Genesis, it says,

> *By the seventh day God had finished the work He had been doing; so on the seventh day He rested from all His work. Then God blessed the seventh day and made it holy, because on it He rested from all the work of creating that He had done.*
>
> —GENESIS 2:2-3

A Day of Delight... A Fresh Beginning!

And several centuries later, the observance of the Sabbath was then, written in stone in the Ten Commandments. The first reading of the Decalogue, or the Law in Exodus, reveals the grounding of the Sabbath in creation.

> *Remember the Sabbath day by keeping it holy... For in six days the Lord made the heavens and the earth, the sea, and all that is in them, but He rested on the seventh day. Therefore, the Lord blessed the Sabbath day and made it holy.*
>
> —EXODUS 20:4

In Deuteronomy, as Moses was preparing the people to enter, possess, and prosper in the Promised Land, he again spoke of the Sabbath. Moses added and urged them to "remember" their deliverance from slavery.

> *Observe the Sabbath day by keeping it holy, as the Lord your God has commanded you... Remember that you were **slaves** in Egypt and that the Lord your God brought you out of there with a mighty hand and an outstretched arm. Therefore, the Lord your God has commanded you to observe the Sabbath day.*
>
> —DEUTERONOMY 5:12, 15, Emphasis Added

God's call for His people to "remember" was a call never to forget that they were once bound in slavery. If you have never been released from your bondage, you do not have a stone of remembrance.[85] If you are still living in bondage to anything, you need to throw off the shackles attached to your past that have kept you "frozen in time!"

God removed all of the obstacles for the children of Israel—from the great plagues to the barrier of the Red Sea. It was necessary that when God said that it was time to go, the people of Israel had to take action by participating in the Passover and then the march to freedom.

By God's decrees and through our willingness to obey those decrees—we form a stone of remembrance so that we can continue on the path of our *transformation*. For our *transformation*, like the Israelites, we must be obedient and participate in God's plan for our own deliverance and freedom.

They needed to remember the pain of their slavery in order to walk into their significant gain of freedom. The history of redemption in the Bible has, at times, been aborted or delayed because man has disobeyed and failed to remember God's instruction to them. When God's Word is first revealed, there is a mighty burst of enthusiasm and zeal, but it can dissipate if we lose focus and fail to follow through. God's call to "remember" is more than a "memory." God's call needs to be translated into action and *transformation*. On the Sabbath, we should take time to "remember" the goodness of God!

THEY NEEDED TO REMEMBER THEIR PAIN OF SLAVERY IN ORDER TO WALK INTO THEIR GREAT GAIN OF FREEDOM.

I *(Phil)* listened to an audiobook on the way to work and heard an interesting story told by Maya Angelou, the famous American poet. She was speaking to a group of ministers who were at a retreat for refreshing and renewal. She told them a story about the slaves in the south. According to her, due to their position as slaves, they were not supposed to laugh or express their joy. So, they developed a tradition that when they *needed* to express laughter, which the Bible says is good medicine, they would find a barrel, place their head inside it, and laugh. This could be an excellent lesson for us. When we are stressed and are in danger of being slaves to this world, we should take a break and remember God's goodness, find a symbolic barrel, and just have a great belly laugh! The rabbi, Abraham Joshua Heschel, says in his book, "It is a sin to be sad on the Sabbath day."[86]

This is a sacred day before our Lord. Don't be dejected and sad, for the joy of the Lord is your strength!

—NEHEMIAH 8:10, NLT

5 RS FOR MAKING YOUR SABBATH DAY A DELIGHT!

*If you keep your feet from breaking the Sabbath and from **doing as you please** (self/soul over spirit) on My holy day, **if** you call the **Sabbath a delight** (spirit ruling over soul), and **if you honor** it by **not going your own way** (not self/soul over spirit) and not doing as you please (not self/soul over spirit) or speaking idle words (self/soul over spirit), **then** you will find your **joy in the Lord**, and I will cause you to **ride in triumph** (Victorious Living!) on the heights of the land.*

—ISAIAH 58:13-14, Brackets and Emphasis Added

The first "R" for making your Sabbath Day a delight is:

1. RELATIONSHIP

While the religious leaders were focused on regulations, Jesus was building relationships. What a contrast! Jesus reminded them that the Sabbath was made for man, not man for the Sabbath. He was proclaiming freedom and rest, and they were entangled in spiritual bondage and man-made rules. Jesus' message must have been a strange paradox and a welcome rest for the weary and overburdened people of that day.

What would it be like if Jesus made a visit on your Sabbath day and you were in chains of despair, obsessed by the cares of the day, ruminating about the past and future, and frantically working to please yourself and God by working harder than you ever have before? What would He say and do? Is your Sabbath about relationship—or about regulations—or non-existent?

Relationship with God is not bondage—it's not carrying a big black Bible with a somber look and wearing dreary clothes and going to a zombie service. It's just being relaxed and having a good time with Jesus, just like you would with the best friend you ever could imagine! The Sabbath should not be filled with worries of condemnation or great expectations but be a time of just hanging out together! It is a time to laugh, to cry, and to dream. This day should not be dull and drab, but fun and fulfilling!

A Day of Delight... A Fresh Beginning!

The second R for making your Sabbath Day a delight:

2. REST

If you are like most of us, your week has probably been a whirlwind of activity. Full of unfinished business, time restraints, pressing agendas, and certainly not enough time for meaningful relationships. With the normal pace of your life, it seems it would be impossible to slow down and catch your breath. Prior to your Sabbath, you need to make a decision to *take action*—to rest!

We need to learn to rest just like God did on His day of rest. God did not rest because He was tired or weary. God selected a day to cease from His own labor and just enjoy everything that He had created. So for us, a true rest involves ceasing from all our self-made activity and just enjoying everything God has created and provided.

Jesus knew the value of getting away and taking a break. He often pulled away from the crowds to rest. Jesus taught us the importance of rest and encouraged us to come to Him as the source for rest.

> *Then Jesus said, "Come to Me, all of you who are weary and carry heavy burdens, and I will give you rest."*
>
> —MATTHEW 11:28

On the Sabbath Day, the religious leaders became extremely restless and angry when they saw Jesus healing the sick. Jesus performed many miracles on the Sabbath, and He was challenged by the religious leaders every time.[87] These challenges led to unrest and strife in these leaders' own lives due to their unwillingness to accept Jesus as the Way, the Truth, and the Life. In contrast, those willing to accept freedom and healing on the Sabbath were set free from their bondage. Talk about a break and real *rest*!

To be *transformed*, we must learn to rest and refuse to return to slavery. Remembering that: "Slaves don't rest. Slaves can't rest. Slaves, by definition, have no freedom to rest. Rest, it turns out, is a condition to liberty."[88]

The third "R" for making your Sabbath Day a delight is:

3. RELEASE and LET IT GO!

Mark Buchanan states, "There is one very large, very grim obstacle to keeping Sabbath. It is the problem of taskmasters. God drowned the taskmasters, it is true—dragged the whole Egyptian army to the muddy, weedy sea's bottom. Only, some survived: they clung to the flotsam (wreckage floating in the sea) of our guilt and worry and ended up marooned in our heads. It's actually worse: we helped them survive. We threw them ropes, pulled them ashore, and resuscitated the unconscious ones. Now, there's a whole noisy, jostling colony of them still with us, and they lapse into old habits the minute we try to rest. They swagger and bark like men in authority—and ought to since we are inclined to give way."[89]

You need to exercise spiritual authority and, "Throw off your Taskmasters!" Who is whipping or controlling you? What is keeping you from your freedom? We can throw away the chains of our old taskmasters because, as the scripture confirms, "So, if the Son sets you free, you are truly free." (John 8:36)

A Day of Delight… A Fresh Beginning!

EXERCISE SPIRITUAL AUTHORITY AND, "THROW OFF YOUR TASKMASTERS!"

To enjoy your Sabbath rest, you must say "No!" to all condemnation! The Sabbath is a time to be free of any words or thoughts of condemnation. If the devil has bullied you throughout the week, harassed you, or made you feel defeated, *this is the day* to declare your freedom in Christ.

> *Therefore, there is now no condemnation for those who are in Christ Jesus, because through Christ Jesus the law of the Spirit who gives life has set you free from the law of sin and death.*
>
> —ROMANS 8:1-2

Each Sabbath is a reminder to keep short accounts against ourselves and others—releasing any blaming, judgments, and criticisms that have inhabited our temple during the week. This requires a weekly Sabbath attitude adjustment!

The fourth "R" for making your Sabbath Day a delight is:

4. RE-EVALUATE and RE-FOCUS!

To quote the famous Dr. Phil (the other one!), "And how is that working for you?" Each week should be a time to "Re-evaluate." Meaning focus on areas that are *not* working and are not aligned with

God's purposes. Your week is driven by your goals and values. Do the goals you set for your day and week attract God's attention and favor? Are you spending your time in meaningful and life-shaping endeavors? Are you choosing *"the one thing"* that is essential? Or are you choosing the *"the many"* that are distracting from your life's purpose?

Each Sabbath, you are given the opportunity to re-evaluate and re-focus by taking time to align your goals and values with God's purpose and His destiny for your life. This provides the atmosphere for *transformation* and renewal.

The fifth "R" for making your Sabbath Day a delight is:

5. REVELATION!

The Holy Spirit brings a fresh *awareness* of God's presence. Revelation comes as we choose to abandon earthly cares and begin to turn our *attention* to God's truth and presence.

The Sabbath is a day to ask for *His* revelation—asking Him to show us new things but also asking Him to remove the veil clouding our current vision and give us a renewed fresh vision.

LET YOUR SABBATH ALWAYS BE A FRESH BEGINNING!

Although I had some understanding of the "Sabbath" principle, I *(Phil)* never completely understood it and all of its ramifications—until I experienced *"THE Happy Dance!"* I realized that for years I had been unaware that there was a deep place in my heart that had been "frozen in time." I had moved on, but the full expression of my personality, my

A Day of Delight… A Fresh Beginning!

relationships, and my ministry could not fully blossom. I had buried a very deep hurt, and it was unrecognizable because it had changed. The negative triad of anxious fear, hidden shame, and emotional pain remained in a place that no one—not even myself—could see.

A heart becomes hardened—or frozen—when individuals experience a trauma, an impossible situation, an unfulfilled desire, or a disappointing or bitter experience. Instead of dealing with your own fear, pain, and shame—you "freeze in time." This life-changing situation becomes too hard for you to handle, and you either run from it, bury it, or put it aside and just keep living your life—unaware that something within you has frozen—and just lingers there waiting to be defrosted!

> **A HEART BECOMES HARDENED—OR FROZEN— WHEN INDIVIDUALS EXPERIENCE A TRAUMA, AN IMPOSSIBLE SITUATION, AN UNFULFILLED DESIRE, OR A DISAPPOINTING OR BITTER EXPERIENCE.**

Outwardly I had moved on, but a very sensitive part of my life was affected and influenced my perception of myself and others I deeply loved. I thought I should be able just to move on. I did not realize that one layer of pain could produce further layers of pain that will ultimately need to be extricated to be fully healed. I have learned that *everyone*, due to our fallen nature, has "frozen" places. Whether our frozen places are mild or severe, they have touched our lives and limited our freedom in Christ.

The negative triad is a signal that something is missing. When your life is paralyzed by unknown *fear* or anxiety, you operate from a different mindset than you would if you were free. When you have unrecognized *shame*, there is a feeling of not measuring up. And exposed *shame* makes us want to cover it up. When you experience hidden emotional *pain*, it prevents you from the full development of your personality and everything that God created you to be. Your spirit, soul, and body become affected by this triad and prevent you from being totally free.

THE NEGATIVE TRIAD IS A SIGNAL THAT SOMETHING IS MISSING.

Jesus offers true rest! What a great day when God reveals to us that there is a path to freedom—He can heal and set us free! We are then able to throw off our taskmasters and anything that has enslaved us—and find our delight in *"THE Happy Dance! It is a day for a new beginning! Refreshed to experience… "THE Happy Dance!"*

My niece, Stephany, was convinced that our Bible study material had to become a book. With her encouragement and gentle pressure—it became a reality. About six months before publication, Mike, Steph's husband, was tragically killed when struck by a vehicle.

Stephany has joyfully embraced and maintained *"THE Happy Dance!"* and declares, *"THE Happy Dance!"* isn't something that just happens once, but it occurs often throughout our lifetime! I have read this book several times, and for each season, it has meant so much! About five years ago, one of the greatest moments of my life was after I had forgiven those who had wounded me, and I had so much freedom that I literally felt as light as a bird!

A Day of Delight... A Fresh Beginning!

I lost my husband in a tragic car accident this year. We were married 18 years and have two beautiful children! Can you *experience "THE Happy Dance"* in the midst of such grief, sorrow and sadness?

My answer is *yes*! Yes, you can! How? By choosing to look for all the fingerprints of God over every little detail! We can't control what happens to us but we can control how we choose to look at the circumstances in life! Is this how I pictured my life going? No way! Knowing that God is sovereign and could have kept my husband from being hit that day, I had to forgive God for not sparing his life. I have seen God in so many details and His presence has been very real even in this season of my life. I want to encourage you, in order to heal, we have to feel and lean into the pain! Even in the trials of life, there are great moments of anticipation and breakthroughs. And *"THE Happy Dance!"* is the way to celebrate!

I like to think of *"THE Happy Dance!"* like a waterfall. When you're under a waterfall you are being hit with new and fresh water from above! When you have *"THE Happy Dance"*, you are celebrating the refreshment, freedom, or revelation that God has given you from above... in those moments, you can't be still... it's time to dance!"

I desire *Victorious* Living... spirit, soul, and body!

I am being TRANSFORMED...
With a Refreshed Heart of Worship
and a Fresh Beginning!

Study Questions

1. Before this study, did you understand the importance of the Sabbath as an opportunity for rest and healing?

    ☐ Yes ☐ No

2. If Jesus made a visit on your Sabbath would He find that you were:

    ☐ In chains of despair

    ☐ Obsessed by the cares of the day

    ☐ Ruminating about the past and future

    ☐ Frantically working to please yourself and GOD by working harder than you ever have before?

    What would He say and do?

    Explain: _____

    _____
    _____
    _____
    _____
    _____

THE Happy Dance

3. Is your Sabbath:

☐ About relationship

☐ About regulations

☐ Non-existent

Explain: _____

_____

_____

_____

_____

_____

_____

4. Why did GOD place such heavy emphasis on remembering the Sabbath day and to keep it holy?

Explain: _____

_____

_____

_____

_____

_____

A Day of Delight... A Fresh Beginning!

5. Check all that apply to your week:

    ☐ Been a whirl-wind of activity

    ☐ Unfinished business

    ☐ Time restraints

    ☐ Pressing agendas

    ☐ Not enough time for important relationships.

6. With the normal pace of your life, it seems it would be impossible to slow down and catch your breath. Prior to your Sabbath Rest, you need to make a decision to *take action*—to rest!

    Are you ready to make this decision?

    ☐ Yes   ☐ No

    Explain: _____

    _____

    _____

    _____

    _____

    _____

7. Man can easily go to extremes. Are you more prone:

    ☐ "too much rest" becoming lethargic

    OR

    ☐ "too much activity" leading to exhaustion.

THE Happy Dance

8. Are you plagued with condemnation or your own inner critic?

   ☐ Yes   ☐ No

9. To enjoy your Sabbath rest, you must say "No!" to all condemnation! All week has the devil bullied you, harassed you, or made you feel defeated?

   ☐ Yes   ☐ No

10. This is the *day* to declare your freedom in Christ! What will this entail?

    Explain: _____

    _____

    _____

    _____

    _____

11. Each week should be a time to "Re-evaluate"—focus on areas that are NOT working and are not aligned with GOD'S purposes. Your week will be driven by your goals and values.

    Do your goals for your day and week attract GOD'S attention and favor?

    ☐ Yes   ☐ No

    Are you spending your time in meaningful and life-shaping endeavors?

    ☐ Yes   ☐ No

Are you choosing "the one thing" that is essential over the "the many" that are distracting from your life's purpose?

☐ Yes ☐ No

12. The negative triad of fear, shame, and pain signals that something is missing. Have you felt their impact?

☐ Yes ☐ No

13. Have you faced:

☐ A trauma

☐ An unfulfilled desire

☐ A bitter experience

☐ An impossible situation

☐ A disappointment

14. Did it cause you to "freeze in time"?

☐ Yes ☐ No

15. This life-changing situation becomes too hard for you to handle. What did you do?

☐ Run from it

☐ Bury it

☐ Put it aside and just keep living your life.

THE Happy Dance

16. God's call for His people to "REMEMBER" was a call to never forget that they were once bound in slavery. Are you are still living in bondage to anything from your past that has kept you "frozen in time!"?

    ☐ Yes   ☐ No

17. Exercise spiritual authority and, "Throw off your Taskmasters!" Who, or what is whipping or controlling you? What is keeping you from your freedom?

    Explain: _____
    _____
    _____
    _____
    _____
    _____
    _____
    _____
    _____

18. Are you willing to dance before the "LORD of the Dance" with a humble heart, demonstrating your need for His grace and mercy, experiencing His deliverance and freedom, and affirming His will and destiny?

    ☐ Yes   ☐ No

Epilogue

I thought this was "past!" This is supposed to be "past!" How do I get "past" this?

It is *not* easy! There is no three-minute fix!

Leaving the residue of your self-made shallow grave of hurt and regret is a process. Because sometimes we need to *remember* so that we can finally forget! But often, the memory is way too painful. And the sorrow, the sadness, the pain… or the anger, resentment, and fear—make us want to shout, "I would rather not 'go' there! I want just to run—run away as Moses and David did in the Bible! Run to a safe place!"

David fled to a cave, and Moses fled to the desert—both wanted to escape personal trauma and find relief and safety there. Sometimes God allows us to run so that we can survive life. But how long should you stay in hiding? God knows what condition your soul is in and how long it will take for it to be restored. God gives you a time of rest for refreshing and refocusing. But before you can leave the desert—you must eventually come face to face with the enemy. But it is God Who will compel the enemy to let you leave—just like he did to Pharaoh! Moses didn't have to create the plagues; he just had to be an instrument of faith. God will deal with the devil—we just have to have faith and put our trust in God!

Before Moses could even think about leaving his desert, he had to put aside his fears. There will be perhaps two fears that will come when you are getting brave enough to move on from "your" desert. Moses experienced these—it was both a fear of rejection (See Exodus 4:1) and a fear of inadequacy (See Exodus 4:10). These fears were conjured up and placed on a silver platter by the devil. Moses took these fears and swallowed them whole. To refute the lies of Satan, God spoke truth to Moses, declaring that He would be enough for Moses to fulfill his destiny (Exodus 4:11).

God is available to lead you because He has just been waiting for you!

> *I have watched over you and have seen what has been done to you... And I have promised to bring you up out of your misery!*
> — EXODUS 3:16,17

As you thaw in your desert, you will no longer be "frozen in time!" And God will redeem and use your desert experience to *transform* you for your destiny!

You will not emerge empty-handed—you will go with your *testimony!*

> *... so that when you leave you will not go empty-handed.*
> —EXODUS 3:21

You must leave your desert so that you can help bring others out of theirs!

Epilogue

"THE HAPPY DANCE!"

There are many steps and moves to *"THE Happy Dance!"* So, as our spirit, soul, and body align with the Holy Spirit, God begins to divulge new intricacies of *"THE Happy Dance!"*

There were the *celebratory steps* of Miriam when they experienced freedom from bondage!

The *exultant steps* of David with the fulfillment of a dream!

The *jubilant steps* of Phil and Debby when we had a *"Happy Dance"* right in the parking lot.

We were all celebrating a fresh beginning—we were all leaving worries and concerns behind us. It was a dance of freedom and celebration!

All of these steps of the Dance were acknowledging God's mighty hand on our life, and we were *rejoicing* with God! It was so easy to rejoice and agree with God —because He agreed *with us*!

But there are many more intricate steps to experience in *"THE Happy Dance!"* Mary, the mother of Jesus, rejoicing. Debby skipping down Ferguson Road. Phil dancing in our living room. These are the intricate steps that we take in *rejoicing and agreeing—with God!* These are the intricate steps toward *transformation*!

Now it is time for your spirit, soul, and body to align. It is time to rejoice and to dance! Let the music begin!

> *I pray that God, who gives peace, will make you completely holy. And may your **spirit**, **soul**, and **body** be kept healthy and faultless until our Lord Jesus Christ returns. The One who chose you can be trusted, and He will do this.*
>
> —1 THESSALONIANS 5:23-24, CEV, Emphasis Added

The Good Shepherd, "The Lord of the Dance", is getting me ready for the ultimate *"Happy Dance!"*

> *For the Lamb at the center of the throne will be their Shepherd; "He will lead them to springs of living water." "And God will wipe away every tear from their eyes."*
>
> —REVELATION 7:17

Finally, we will be **totally** *Transformed!*

> *You have turned my mourning into joyful dancing. You have taken away my clothes of mourning and clothed me with joy, that I might sing praises to You and not be silent. O Lord my God, I will give You thanks forever!*
>
> —PSALM 30:11-12 NLT

As the host of angels begin its angelic chorus, "The Lord of the Dance" extends His hand, *"May I have this Dance?"*

I step forward with joy in my heart because the steps to this Dance I know—It is *"THE Happy Dance!"*

STEP 1— I have been TRANSFORMED...
  By Not Settling to Be the Average Christian!

STEP 2— I have been TRANSFORMED...
  By Being Set Free!

STEP 3— I have been TRANSFORMED...
  By Being Brave!
  By Being Honest!

By Being Humble!
By Being Grateful!

STEP 4— I have been *TRANSFORMED*...
By Taking Action to Be Free!

STEP 5— I have been *TRANSFORMED*...
By Pulling Down My Stronghold!

STEP 6— I have been *TRANSFORMED*...
By Learning to Trust God!

STEP 7— I have been *TRANSFORMED*...
By Burning My Trash!
By Being Healed— Spirit, Soul, and Body!

STEP 8— I have been *TRANSFORMED*...
By Becoming a Living Sacrifice—Spirit, Soul, and Body!

STEP 9— I have been *TRANSFORMED*...
By Making Godly Decisions!

STEP 10— I have been *TRANSFORMED*...
By Being a Good Steward Serving the Creator, Instead of the Creature!

STEP 11— I have been *TRANSFORMED*...
With A Refreshed Heart of Worship and A Fresh Beginning!

Endnotes

CHAPTER ONE

1. See Mark 10:17-23
2. New American Standard New Testament Greek Lexicon
3. AZ Quotes.com
4. QuotesGram.com
5. See 2 Timothy 2:21 ESV
6. HELPS Word-studies
7. Watchman Nee, *The Spiritual Man Volume One*, (New York: Christian Fellowship Publishers, Inc., 1968), 26.
8. Christopher Lasch, *The Culture of Narcissism: American Life in an Age of Diminishing Expectations.*

CHAPTER TWO

9. Watchman Nee, *The Spiritual Man Volume Two*, (New York: Christian Fellowship Publishers, Inc., 1968), 71.
10. IBID.
11. See Revelation 12:10
12. See Isaiah 49:16
13. See 2 Kings 5:14
14. See 2 Samuel 6:14
15. Lyrics by Patt Barrett and Anthony Brown

CHAPTER THREE

16 Encarta Dictionary
17 Cambridge Dictionary
18 Merriam-Webster Dictionary
19 HELPS Word-studies
20 See Exodus 15:20
21 Lyrics by Patt Barrett and Anthony Brown

CHAPTER FOUR

22 See 1 Corinthians 2:16
23 See Romans 8:6
24 Romans 8:7
25 See Romans 1:25
26 Encarta Dictionary
27 IBID.
28 IBID.
29 IBID.
30 See Psalm 139:14
31 See Matthew 5:3

CHAPTER FIVE

32 HELPS Word Studies
33 Thayer Greek Lexicon
34 HELPS Word Studies
35 David Wilkerson Devotions, *"Dealing with our Strongholds,"* July 23, 2009
36 HELPS Word Studies
37 IBID.
38 Rick Hanson, *Hardwiring Happiness*, (New York: Harmony Books, 2013).

CHAPTER SIX

39 See Jeremiah 7:9
40 *DSM 5*, (Washington D.C.: American Psychiatric Association, 2013), 659
41 See 1 Peter 3:6

Endnotes

42 Ephesians 4:26
43 Dr. Robert Berezin, *Do No Harm: The Destructive History of Pharmaceutical Psychiatry and its Bedfellows-Electroshock, Insulin Shock, and Lobotomies*, 271.

CHAPTER SEVEN

44 H, J Eysenck, "Personality, Stress, and Anger: Prediction and Prophylaxis," *British Journal of Medical Psychology*, 61 (1988): 57-75
45 M. A Mittleman, M. Manclure, J. B. Sherwood, et al., "Triggering of Acute Myocardial Infarction Onset of Episodes of Anger," *Circulation*, 92 (1995): 1720-1725.
46 B. Hafen, K. Frandsen, K. Karen, et. al., *The Health Effects of Attitudes, Emotions, and Relationship* (Provo, Utah: EMS Associates, 1992).
47 A. Hart, *Adreneline and Stress* (Nashville: W Publishing Group, 1995)
48 Holistic Dentistry
49 Don Colbert MD, *Deadly Emotions*, (Nashville: Thomas Nelson Publishers, 2003), 16.
50 IBID.,17
51 IBID.,18
52 IBID.,25
53 IBID.,25-27
54 Doc Childre and Howard Martin, *The HeartMath Solution*, (San Francisco: HarperCollins, 1999), 55.
55 IBID.
56 Peter A. Levine, PhD, *In an Unspoken Voice*, (Berkeley, North Atlantic Books, 2010), 45.

CHAPTER EIGHT

57 www.verywell.com
58 Vertex LLC42
59 verywell.com
60 IBID
61 IBID
62 David Kessler, *The End of Overeating*, (New York: Rodale, 2009), 7.
63 IBID., 7

64	IBID., 8
65	IBID., 10
66	IBID., 14
67	IBID., 21
68	IBID., 37
69	IBID., 139
70	IBID., 140
71	IBID., 153
72	IBID., 249
73	IBID.
74	www.FrederickBuechner.com
75	Travis Bradberry, FORBES
76	Thayer's Greek Lexicon

CHAPTER NINE

77	Wikipedia
78	Ann Streissguth, *Fetal Alcohol Syndrome*, (Baltimore: Paul H. Brookes Publishing Co, 1997) 6.
79	Ibid.
80	See 2 Corinthians 10:5
81	See Matthew 7:14

CHAPTER TEN

82	Encarta Dictionary
83	Dallas Willard, *Renovation of the Heart*, (Colorado Springs: NavPress Books, 2002), 159.
84	C.S. Lewis, *Mere Christianity*, (New York: Harper Collins, 1952). 176.

CHAPTER ELEVEN

85	See Joshua 4:1-9
86	Abraham Joshua Heschel, *The Sabbath*, (New York: Farrar, Straus and Giroux, 1951), 31.
87	See Matthew 12; Mark 3; Luke 6; Luke 13; John 7:2; John 9:14.
88	Mark Buchanan, *The Rest of God*, (Nashville: W Publishing Group, Thomas Nelson, 2006), 90.
89	Ibid.